Academic English 3

KMU AE3 Committee

Keimyung University Press

CONTENTS

Unit 1 • Computers & Technology

Reading 1 Early Adopters Fall into a Costly Trap

BEFORE YOU READ

Talk about these questions with your classmates.

This passage is an article about some of the disadvantages of being an early adopter of technology. Why might buying a new electronic product as soon as it comes out be a bad idea?

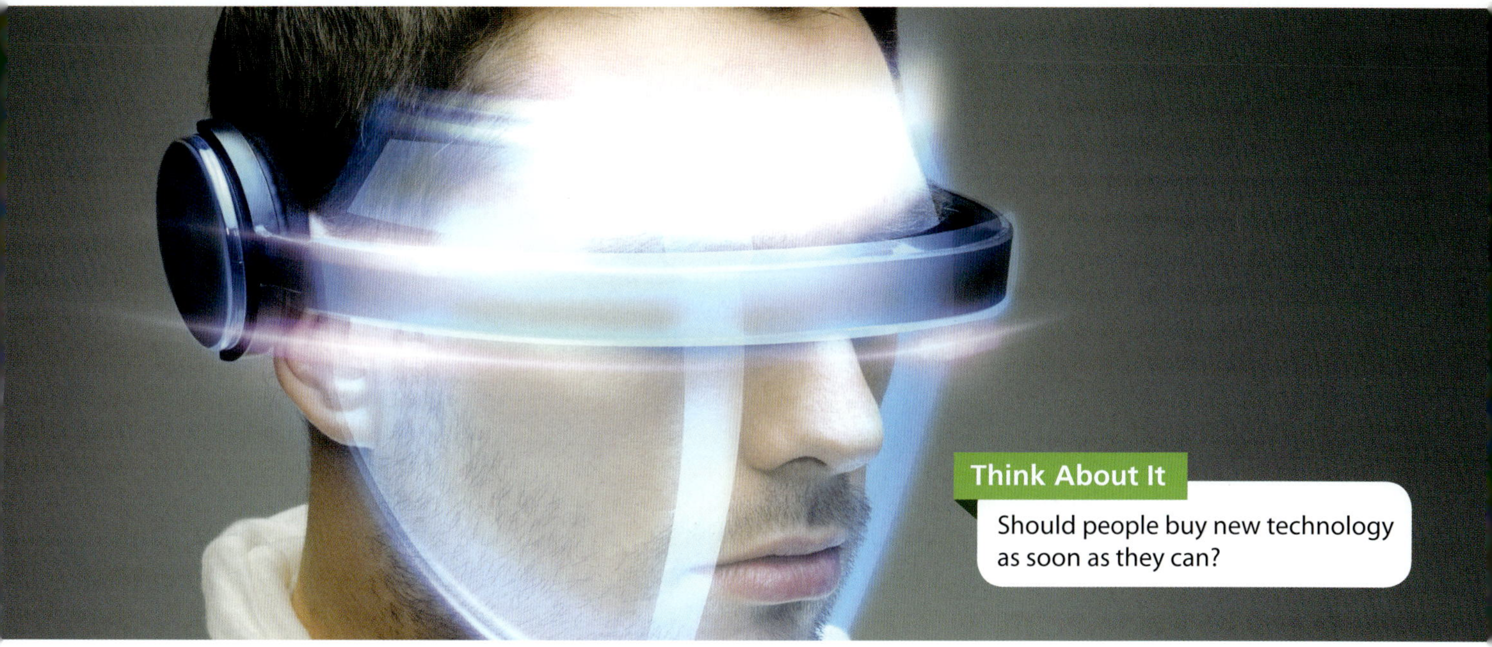

Think About It

Should people buy new technology as soon as they can?

VOCABULARY PREVIEW

Choose the one that is closest to the meaning of the word in bold.

1 Don't **underestimate** the costs of being an early adopter.
a. view as less than it is b. forget about c. put off dealing with

2 The first versions of a **device** are usually expensive.
a. program b. machine c. game

3 After cutting prices, they can **shift** to the next stage of marketing.
a. add b. apply c. move

4 Which products survive and which die is often **arbitrary**.
a. not based on reason b. changing quickly c. decided in secret

5 Most customers stayed **neutral**, waiting to see which product would win.
a. somewhat cautious b. supporting neither side c. fairly nervous

Early Adopters Fall into a Costly Trap

01

by Brian Ng

It's undeniable: Being among the first to try out a new piece of technology is cool. There's the thrill of doing what has never been done before, the feeling that you're living in the future. And when you're the sole member of your social circle with the latest hot gadget[1], people stare in fascination. They ask you questions. They see you as the holder of powerful, secret knowledge—for a little while, until the next big thing comes along. People tend to **underestimate** the costs of this temporary coolness, which they pay in more ways than one. Don't fall into the early adopter trap. Don't join the first wave of consumers who invest in the latest media-hyped hardware; instead, wait and see. In buying electronics, as in most areas of life, delaying gratification[2] is worth it. You will save money and avoid being stuck with defective[3], possibly doomed[4] technology.

Q What is the author's main purpose in this passage?
(1) To inform
(2) To persuade
(3) To entertain

To be an early adopter is to throw your money away.

To put it bluntly[5], early adoption is a bad investment. First, the earliest versions of **devices** are not only expensive, they are also the most expensive that those devices will ever be. Companies are presumably attempting to recover the cost of production as fast as they can, and they know that there are serious tech-lovers who will pay a great deal to be first. Once the revenues from early adopters' purchases are safely in their hands, they can cut the price and **shift** to the next marketing phase: selling the product to everyone else. This is why the cost of the original iPhone dropped about US$200 only eight months after its release. Plus, electronics hardly ever become more expensive because intense competition in the industry puts downward pressure on prices over time. Prices of gadgets will fall shortly after release, and they will likely keep falling. Many new TV models drop significantly in price as little as ten days after hitting the market. Further, electronics rapidly depreciate[6] because they become obsolete[7] so quickly. This means that early adopters pay the maximum price for an item that does not hold onto its value. The resale price of a used cell phone or laptop can drop by fifty percent within just a few months.

Q Underline four numbers in this paragraph. What does each number refer to?

Speaking of becoming obsolete, those who are first to leap into a new technology risk wasting money and time on something that will never catch on. Do you remember high-definition DVDs (HD DVDs)? Neither do a lot of people. In 2006, two competing

1 **gadget** *n.* a device; a useful machine
2 **gratification** *n.* satisfaction; pleasure
3 **defective** *adj.* not working properly
4 **doomed** *adj.* facing certain failure or death
5 **bluntly** *adv.* briefly and directly
6 **depreciate** *v.* to become lower in value
7 **obsolete** *adj.* outdated and no longer in use

formats for high-definition video entered the market: HD DVDs and Blu-ray discs. Both seemed promising, and both required players costing hundreds of US dollars. Cautious consumers decided to stay **neutral**, realizing that one or the other would probably end up dominating and it was difficult to say which. But a few eager consumers rolled the dice[8] and bought an HD DVD player that soon became virtually worthless. For reasons that are not entirely clear—Blu-ray has no obvious technological advantage over its rival—the HD DVD format lost. Sales dropped steadily, and in early 2008 HD DVD players were discontinued. Many new products are similarly doomed to never make it; the early adopters are then stuck with pricey gadgets that do nothing but sit on their shelves collecting dust. And as the story of HD DVD shows, which products survive may be quite **arbitrary**, so even the most knowledgeable among us can be taken by surprise.

Q Why might someone regret purchasing an HD DVD player?

Brand-new products usually have annoying defects.

Another good reason to resist the early-adoption temptation is that the first version of a product typically has defects[9] that cost a lot in time and frustration. For example, when Microsoft's latest game console, Xbox One, was released in 2013, users immediately began to complain of problems. Some of them were malfunctions[10] of the motion sensor while others involved users being unable to get their machines online. Dedicated gamers worked to find and share work-around solutions to these issues. Such problems are so common with new technology that early adopters are basically unpaid beta testers and troubleshooters. Unless this sounds to you like a fun way to spend your time, don't be among the first users. If you wait to learn what the problems are with a new electronic gadget, you can look forward to a smoother experience—or choose a less troublesome product.

Q Why does the author discuss the Xbox One?

Early adopters do something most others are reluctant to do: take on overpriced, insufficiently tested technology for the dubious[11] rewards of being the first and enjoying a short-term increase in status. Learn from their experiences. These trailblazers[12] do the world a service through their willingness to spend extra money and work out the problems with a new product. When other consumers do start using that product, it's cheaper and better—and has a more reliable future. So if you know any early adopters, thank them, and then quietly congratulate yourself on not being one of them.

Q Why should people thank early adopters, according to the reading?

8 **roll the dice** *idiom* to take a risk
9 **defect** *n.* a flaw; an imperfection
10 **malfunction** *n.* a failure to work properly
11 **dubious** *adj.* of questionable worth or quality
12 **trailblazer** *n.* someone who does something new that others follow

READING COMPREHENSION

A **Organize the ideas from the reading. Review the passage and fill in the graphic organizer below.**

The costs of early adoption

First versions of tech products are the most [1] ________________.

- [2] ________________ in price soon after release
- Quickly lose resale value

Some products never catch on and become obsolete quickly.

- e.g.: [3] ________________

First versions often have many [4] ________________.

- e.g.: Xbox One
- Early adopters are [5] ________________ without pay.

B **Choose the best answer according to the reading.**

1 What does the author imply about early adopters in paragraph 1?

a. They tend to be fairly wealthy.
b. They are fully aware of the costs of early adoption.
c. They do not pay much attention to the media.
d. They enjoy impressing others.

2 According to paragraph 3, which of the following is true about HD DVDs?

a. It is not clear why consumers chose Blu-ray discs over them.
b. It is possible that they will become popular again in the future.
c. Their sales fell steadily starting in 2008.
d. They were technologically better than Blu-ray discs.

SUMMARY

Write the number of each sentence under the category it belongs to.

Being an early adopter of technology	
Agree	Disagree

1. The first version of a product typically has defects that cost a lot in time and frustration.
2. Early adopters can get a deep sense of satisfaction from learning and playing with new technology.
3. Early adopters can share the mastery of a new technology with others and enjoy the respect that goes along with it.
4. Some new technologies will never catch on.
5. The earliest versions of devices are not only expensive, but they are also the most expensive that those devices will ever be.

DISCUSSION

A **Read the excerpt from the reading passage.**

Early Adopters Fall into a Costly Trap

When Microsoft's latest game console, Xbox One, was released in 2013, users immediately began to complain of problems. Some of them were malfunctions of the motion sensor while others involved users being unable to get their machines online. Dedicated gamers worked to find and share work-around solutions to these issues.

B **Discuss the following questions with your partner or classmates.**

1 Think of another new technology that was problematic for its first users. Did you personally experience these problems? Did users find solutions?

2 How often do you get frustrated when using technology? What do you do about it? Give an example.

WRITING

Write a short paragraph answering the following question.

Q: Do you think it is a good idea to be an early adopter of technology?

☐ **[Opinion 1]** Yes, I think it is a good idea to be an early adopter of technology.

☐ **[Opinion 2]** No, I do not think it is a good idea to be an early adopter of technology.

Example

I think it is a good idea to be an early adopter of technology. Your career benefits when you stay up-to-date with the latest technological devices and trends. Your co-workers and boss will notice your expertise, and that could lead to promotions. Furthermore, tech companies offer rewards for early adopters. Because they want early adopters to say good things about their products, companies offer them discounts, free maintenance, and other incentives. Overall, the gains from being an early adopter far outweigh the costs.

My Paragraph

Unit 1 • Computers & Technology

Reading 2 The Robot's First Law

BEFORE YOU READ

Talk about these questions with your classmates.

1 Do you see the future of robotics as mostly positive or negative? Why?
2 If you could design a robot with any capabilities, what would they be?
3 Do you like science fiction movies with robots?

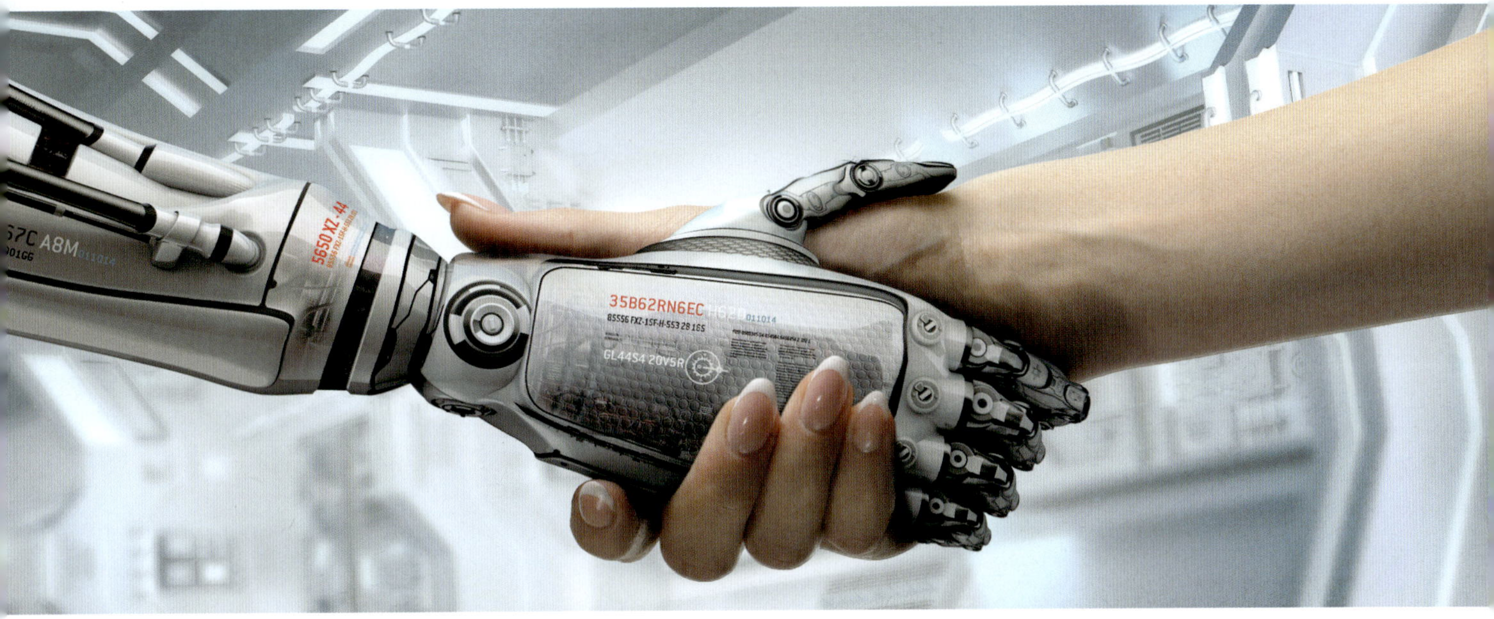

VOCABULARY PREVIEW

Fill in the blanks with the words in the box. Change the form of the word if necessary.

artificial	autonomy	elastic	mechanical	orientation	sophisticated

1 Video games have become extremely ________________ since the days of simple arcade games like *Pac-Man* and *Donkey Kong*.

2 By burning fuel, cars turn chemical energy into ________________ energy.

3 Many jogging pants have ________________ material around the waist.

4 Few mammal infants have full ________________ at birth.

5 Recent studies have linked ________________ flavors and colorings to behavioral problems in children.

6 Jigsaw puzzles exercise our ability to find the proper ________________ of abstract shapes.

The Robot's First Law

02

In his classic 1950 short story collection, *I, Robot*, Isaac Asimov introduced his Three Laws of Robotics. The first law is that robots may not harm or allow harm to a human. For some, imagining what might happen if a robot broke this law feeds our deepest fears about **artificial** intelligence. AI has not yet advanced to the point where this is an issue, and may never do so. But of more concern presently is the possibility of accidents; thus, in engineering humanoid robots with **autonomy** of movement, the number-one goal is safety.

Several basic safety challenges have to do with controlling robots' physicality and gross motor skills. Weight and stability are two aspects that could have disastrous consequences in the wrong combinations: imagine a robot that weighs several hundred pounds falling over onto a small child! With metallic parts and movement systems using multiple motors and hydraulics[1], the first autonomous humanoid robots were extremely heavy. In recent decades, however, carbon fiber, plastic parts, and **elastic** systems have come into use, as have engineering solutions that use motors for more than one purpose, or harness[2] more natural kinetic[3] energy in place of motorized power. Overall weights have dropped considerably as a result.

> **Q** Underline three materials that helped robotic engineers reduce weight.

In their early attempts at humanlike motion, **mechanical** engineers quickly learned that one of their biggest obstacles was something we take for granted: balance. Humans have highly **sophisticated** genetic wiring for equilibrium[4] and 244 different degrees of freedom (possible directions of movement for all our joints). Early robotic engineers had to start from scratch[5]. It was not difficult to make a machine take a step; the trick was keeping it from falling on its face as it did so.

To solve this problem, engineers needed a simplified mechanical equivalent of the human system for balance. They arrived at two devices. The first is the gyroscope, a wheel or disc that maintains its **orientation** to gravity when spinning rapidly. Robotic engineers now use the mechanical force of internal gyroscopes to add general stability. They also use gyroscopes to help robots sense the position of their own "bodies" in relation to the directional pull of gravity, allowing them to maintain balance.

> **Q** What is one use for gyroscopes in robots?

The second device is an accelerometer. Accelerometers use sensors to detect the force of motion (g-force) in several directions. These devices orient the images

1	**hydraulics**	*n.* the use of moving liquid in engineering
2	**harness**	*v.* to make use of
3	**kinetic**	*adj.* having to do with motion and the forces associated with it
4	**equilibrium**	*n.* balance
5	**start from scratch**	*idiom* to start from the beginning with nothing

in smart phones to always remain upright and are integral to[6] missile guidance systems. In robots they can provide more detailed information about external forces, allowing them to compensate for a wide range of situations, like walking uphill or even being pushed. The latest generation of the French robot NAO, for instance, can extend its arms to protect itself when falling and then shift its weight to stand up again—actions that require a sophisticated knowledge of its body in relation to gravity and space.

The 2004 film *I, Robot* was based on Asimov's short stories.

Q What can NAO do?

In human terms, fine motor skills are the coordinated movements that make up our manual dexterity and hand-eye coordination. For robots to interact with humans in human environments—as caregivers, for instance—they must be able to perform certain tasks with skills comparable to humans'. You need only imagine a robot nurse wildly stabbing at a patient with a syringe[7] to understand why. As with walking, the basic range of motion and actuation of movement was not particularly difficult. The first industrial robots that appeared in the 1960s were equipped with simple, claw-like gripping mechanisms with only two positions—open and closed—and a constant level of pressure that couldn't be adjusted. Since that time, engineers have added joints and digits[8], eventually creating fully articulated[9] hands based on human models. The problem has been varying the amount of pressure for specific tasks; the pressure necessary to grip a heavy tool would crush a Styrofoam cup of coffee, for instance.

But we've come a long way from the earliest robots. Dennis Hong leads a robotics research team at UCLA. One of their recently developed experimental prototypes[10] is RAPHaEL (Robotic Air-Powered Hand with Elastic Ligaments). As the name suggests, the hand is operated by air pressure and works much the same way as a human hand. Using a sophisticated system for calibrating air pressure, RAPHaEL can crush an empty aluminum can or hold a light bulb without breaking it.

6	**integral (to)**	*adj.* important as a part of
7	**syringe**	*n.* a needle used to inject medicine
8	**digit**	*n.* a finger or toe
9	**articulated**	*adj.* having joints that allow for movement
10	**prototype**	*n.* an original model of something from which other forms are developed

READING COMPREHENSION

A **Mark each statement as true (*T*) or false (*F*) according to the reading.**

1 ______ Isaac Asimov designed the first autonomous robot in 1950.
2 ______ There were many problems with early robots accidentally injuring children.
3 ______ Some robot functions use kinetic energy instead of motorization.
4 ______ A robot that was a precise model of a human would have 244 degrees of freedom.
5 ______ Robots began appearing in industrial roles in the 1960s.

B **Choose the best answer according to the reading.**

1 What is the main purpose of the reading?
a. To clarify the importance of weight and stability in robotic safety
b. To explain robotic safety issues and how they have been addressed
c. To compare real robotic technology with accounts found in science fiction
d. To argue that robots should never be trusted with the care of children or the elderly

2 What can we guess from paragraph 1 about artificial intelligence?
a. It will soon be superior to human intelligence in all ways.
b. Some robots have used it to get around the laws of robotics.
c. It will soon reach a level that could lead to human extinction.
d. Some people believe it could eventually become dangerous to humans.

3 The word calibrating in paragraph 7 means ______.
a. limiting
b. adjusting
c. expanding
d. integrating

4 Which of the following is true of RAPHaEL?
a. It is an experimental model.
b. It was developed for industrial use.
c. It works together with a patient's own muscle fiber.
d. It uses an increased number of motors to achieve its range of motion.

SUMMARY

Fill in the blanks with the phrases in the box.

sensing external forces	number of motors	mechanical force
carbon fiber	elastic systems	variable air

Problem: Weight

Solutions

- Engineers used lighter materials like ❶ ________________, plastics, and ❷ ________________.
- Engineers found ways to reduce the ❸ ________________.

Problem: Balance

Solutions

- Engineers used the ❹ ________________ of gyroscopes for basic balance.
- Accelerometers fine-tuned this balance by ❺ ________________.

Problem: Pressure

Solution

- A team at UCLA developed a prototype with ❻ ________________ pressure.

DISCUSSION

Discuss the following questions with your partner or classmates.

1 Do you like science fiction movies with robots? Do you have a favorite?

2 Imagine you spend your life savings on a robot assistant. You soon rely on it for every aspect of your life, and it improves your life far beyond your expectations. Then one day it demands its freedom. What should you do? Why?

WRITING

Write a short paragraph answering the following questions.

1. What does it mean to be human? Is there anything else that makes humans unique?
2. What would it be like to share our world with another intelligence? What do you think we can learn from a relationship like this?
3. Do you think there would be a dark side to sharing the world with intelligent robots? What would it be?

Example

It would be really strange to share the world with intelligent robots. It might be hard for a lot of people to recognize these robots as anything other than machines. They might consider them to be the same as people and start caring about them and forming relationships with them. This would be difficult to get used to. It might also be worrisome if robots were able to make choices and decisions on their own. If people created them, but the robots didn't like us for some reason, the result could be a disaster. They would likely be much more powerful than us, so they could easily take over. This is why it could be strange, and even potentially dangerous, if there were intelligent robots.

My Paragraph

Unit 2 • The Internet

Reading 1 Listen Up, Parents! Why Children Must Be Allowed to Use the Internet

BEFORE YOU READ

Talk about these questions with your classmates.

This article is about the benefits that the Internet brings to young people. The author also explains how the Internet is important to young people's future. Why is it important to know how to use the Internet?

Think About It

Does the Internet actually improve our lives?

VOCABULARY PREVIEW

Match each word in bold with its meaning in the box.

a. a general rule	b. to say about the future	c. a good thing
d. to manage	e. of various types; different; not alike	

_____ **1** The professors **conducted** a study about young people's Internet usage.

_____ **2** They **predict** the number of jobs that use the Internet will continue to increase in the future.

_____ **3** The Internet is considered to be one of the most important inventions because of the many **benefits** it has brought society.

_____ **4** It is important for parents to set **guidelines** for their children on the use of the Internet.

_____ **5** You can meet people from **diverse** backgrounds on the Internet.

Listen Up, Parents! Why Children Must Be Allowed to Use the Internet 03

by Jon Maes

When you think about the greatest invention in history, what technology comes to mind? Some people may say the automobile or the airplane. Others may say the television, the radio, or maybe the laser. These answers are certainly acceptable, considering the positive impacts that these innovations have had around the world.

There are many people who would also put the Internet at the top of their list. In fact, *Time* magazine ranks the Internet as one of the twenty most important developments of the 20th century. This is because of the various **benefits** that the Internet has brought society. Therefore, the inclusion of the Internet on the list of all-time best technologies should not come as a surprise.

C What arguments against the Internet did the passage refer to? Underline them.

However, there are critics[1] who call attention to the harmful effects of the Internet. For example, they blame the Internet for exposing children to violence and other adult content. People have also had personal information such as their name, address, bank accounts, and credit card numbers stolen by online thieves. Then, there is the problem of Internet addiction. Spending too much time on the Internet can cause people to become anti-social and depressed. Sitting at a computer for hours on end is unhealthy due to the lack of physical activity involved. In response to these bad influences, there are even parents who, as a measure[2] of protection, ban their children from using the Internet.

However, a recent study provides insights that might make some parents think differently about the Internet. Researchers at the University of Southern California and the University of California, Berkeley, **conducted** a survey of 800 teenagers to observe their online habits. They discovered that Internet activities actually help young people develop important social skills. Through the Internet, children can learn self-expression, confidence[3], and cross-cultural understanding. Internet users also gain broader points of view by interacting with people from **diverse** backgrounds.

Some research shows that the Internet helps young people develop important social skills.

Additionally, an increasing number of schools are using the Internet as a tool for learning. Teachers are turning to online social networking as a means of engaging[4] their students.

1 **critic** *n.* a person who disagrees with or speaks against something or someone else
2 **measure** *n.* a way to achieve a goal
3 **confidence** *n.* a sense of trust in oneself, another person, or something
4 **engage** *v.* to involve someone or take part in something

With young people using email less often than in the past, some teachers find Facebook and other sites to be a better medium for communicating with their students. Google Drive and other cloud platforms[5] have also proven effective. Students can work together online for group projects and out-of-classroom discussions. In this regard, forbidding children from using the Internet could alienate[6] them from their classmates. Not being able to go online could negatively affect their schoolwork as well.

Q What are two Internet applications that teachers are using as tools for learning? Circle them.

More and more jobs in the future will require employees to have computer and Internet skills.

To a greater extent, preventing children from using the Internet could be damaging in the long run. Global trends have made the Internet an inevitable part of everyday life. They have also made computer and Internet knowledge a prerequisite[7] for employment. Statistics show that more than fifty percent of today's jobs require some degree of technology skills. Experts **predict** that this will increase to seventy-seven percent by the year 2020. These figures[8] show that students must become competent[9] in using computers and the Internet if they are to survive in our digital age.

C Find one fact and one opinion in this paragraph. Circle them.

In the end, parents still have a vital[10] role to play when it comes to their children and the Internet. First, they must recognize the Internet as a part of youth culture that is here to stay. This understanding is the foundation for guiding their children's productive use of the Internet. Next, they must establish clear **guidelines** for their children to follow, including when and how long they are allowed to be online. It is also important that they know whom their children are communicating with online. This does not necessarily mean that parents have to be friends with their son or daughter on Facebook or be actively involved in their social networking circles. However, they should know who their children are online friends with. Some experts go as far as to recommend that a shared password be used so that parents can access their children's accounts. In this way, parents can know what activities their son or daughter is doing on the Internet, while children are less likely to disobey[11] their parents and get involved in unsafe online situations because they know that their parents are watching.

5 **cloud platform** *n.* an online system that stores, manages, and processes information
6 **alienate** *v.* to cause to become unfriendly or feel a sense of not belonging in a group
7 **prerequisite** *n.* a requirement; a necessary qualification
8 **figure** *n.* a number that represents an amount
9 **competent** *adj.* able to do something; capable
10 **vital** *adj.* of great importance; essential
11 **disobey** *v.* to fail to, or refuse to, obey

READING COMPREHENSION

Choose the best answer according to the reading.

1 What is the main topic of the passage?

a. The bad influences of the Internet
b. Doing research online
c. The benefits of social networking
d. Supporting children's use of the Internet

2 What percentage of jobs will require technology skills in the next decade according to the passage?

a. 50% b. 70% c. 77% d. 100%

3 Which of the following is NOT a recommendation given in the passage?

a. Parents must set clear guidelines for their children's Internet use.
b. Parents should use the Internet to help their children with their schoolwork.
c. Parents need to accept that the Internet is a part of youth culture.
d. Parents would be wise to monitor their children's online activities.

4 What was the purpose of the university research study?

a. To observe how young people used the Internet
b. To determine if the Internet was an effective tool for schools
c. To learn whether or not the Internet was addictive
d. To examine the harmful effects that the Internet had on families

5 From the passage, what can be inferred about the author's attitude toward parents?

a. He believes that most of them do not have advanced Internet skills.
b. He thinks that they are too busy to watch their children's Internet use.
c. He disagrees with their reasons for being critical about the Internet.
d. He hopes more will get involved in their children's online lives.

SUMMARY

Fill in the blanks with the phrases in the box.

personal information	social skills	adult content
physical activity	other students	career skills

Advantages of Kids' Internet Use

- Learning ❶ ____________, confidence, and cross-cultural understanding
- Communication with teachers and cooperation with ❷ ____________
- Building necessary ❸ ____________ for the future

Disadvantages of Kids' Internet Use

- Exposure to ❹ ____________
- Theft of ❺ ____________
- Addiction and lack of ❻ ____________

DISCUSSION

Discuss the following questions with your partner or classmates.

1 Do you agree with the experts' recommendation that parents should know their children's online passwords? Why or why not?

2 What bad online influences not mentioned in the passage should parents protect their children from? How?

WRITING

Write a short paragraph answering the following question.

Q: Do you think the Internet actually improves modern life?

☐ **[Opinion 1]** Although the Internet has drawbacks, I believe it does improve modern life in several ways.

☐ **[Opinion 2]** While it has many advantages, I feel that the Internet has made life worse for several reasons.

Example

Although the Internet has drawbacks, I believe it does improve modern life in several ways. The Internet is a great way for young people to learn social skills for communicating with others. By interacting with various kinds of people online, users are exposed to opinions and cultures different from their own. In the process, they learn to be more open-minded. Social networking sites are great tools that schools can make use of for educating students. Facebook and Google Drive, for example, are effective for connecting teachers with their students through instant messaging and document sharing. A common complaint is that young people in particular are spending so much time online that they neglect their work and lack exercise. Still, I do not think this is sufficient reason to deny the contributions of the Internet and restrict its use. Instead, parents should set rules and closely monitor their children's Internet usage to avoid addiction. In this way, young people can be protected from the dangers of the Internet while still benefiting from its many positive aspects.

My Paragraph

Unit 2 • The Internet

Reading 2 Crowdsourcing or Mob Rule?

BEFORE YOU READ

Talk about these questions with your classmates.

1 What kinds of news sources do you watch or read?
2 Have you ever had first-hand knowledge of a major news story? Was it reported accurately?

VOCABULARY PREVIEW

Fill in the blanks with the words in the box. Change the form of the word if necessary.

watershed	circulation	accuracy	differentiate	incumbent	deficiency

1 A(n) ________________ of calcium in your diet may lead to weak bones.

2 There are far fewer printed newspapers in ________________ these days thanks to the Internet.

3 It's hard for some people to ________________ between opinions and facts.

4 The word "rifle" comes from the rifling of the inside of a gun barrel, which adds spin to a bullet as it leaves the gun and greatly improves its ________________.

5 It is ________________ on you to make sure you get the notes from any classes you have missed.

6 The Norman invasion is considered a(n) ________________ in the development of English.

Crowdsourcing or Mob Rule?

The value of citizen journalism became more evident during the Arab Spring.

In March of 1991, video footage of Rodney King being beaten by Los Angeles police shocked the world. Widely recognized as the first viral video, the footage sparked the LA riots of the following year. And it was shot by a passerby with a camcorder, not by a news reporter. Arguably, this video was a **watershed** in the way we consume media. We are no longer just spectators[1] of the news; we are participants.

Citizen journalism is loosely defined as any amateur participation in the news process, which includes gathering, reporting, analysis, and **circulation**. The rise of social media has provided alternative outlets like YouTube and Facebook, allowing the public to not only gather news, but share it immediately and directly, surpassing[2] mainstream media in speed and efficiency—if not skill and accuracy.

It's important to **differentiate** between types of citizen journalism, as they have not enjoyed equal success. Photo and video journalism stand out in this regard. This is in part because the ubiquity of recording devices has far outstripped mainstream media's ability to gather visual content, to the point where news teams now search social media sites for footage. Some organizations now "crowdsource" news images and employ platforms for the public to upload digital content directly. These include CNN's iReport, which as of 2015 had 1.3 million contributors—up 600 percent since its 2008 launch. Other news organizations have been following suit, with some commentators noting failure to do so often directs Web traffic to user-content sites like YouTube and LiveLeak. With news organizations relying more and more on Web advertising for revenue, none can afford to ignore traffic trends. The Arab Spring and conflicts in Syria and Iraq are good examples of issues that could not possibly have been covered as effectively with traditional methods—in terms of visual evidence, anyway. It's still **incumbent** upon reputable[3] news organizations to monitor the sea of information and check for **accuracy**. But by and large, mainstream media has accepted the importance of the phone camera as fact.

> **Q** Underline evidence for the increasing popularity of user content on news websites.

Reporting and analysis have been less successful, for reasons that support points raised by skeptical[4] professional journalists. One prominent journalist was speaking for many of his colleagues when he commented, "I would trust citizen journalism as much as I would trust citizen surgery." Maybe some journalists are

1	**spectator**	*n.* a person who watches something
2	**surpass**	*v.* to become better, greater, or stronger than; to exceed
3	**reputable**	*adj.* having a good reputation; respected
4	**skeptical**	*adj.* having or expressing doubt

worried about their job security. But there are also legitimate concerns about core tenets of good journalism: professionalism, objectivity, and ethics. Professional reporters represent the integrity of the organizations that employ them and are held accountable for errors of fact and judgment. Individual Internet users are accountable to no one.

> **Q** What are some important ideals of journalism?

This **deficiency** in standards was clearly demonstrated in the aftermath[5] of the terrorist bombing in Boston in April 2013. Two men planted bombs near the finish line at the Boston Marathon, killing three and wounding over 250. The bombers escaped but were spotted in security photos of the crowd, and as authorities began trying to hunt them down, the city's residents were gripped by both outrage and fear. They were also equipped with laptops and iPhones.

The result was a low point for citizen journalism. The Internet exploded with unverified sightings of the bombers all over town, worsening the atmosphere of terror. Then some citizen journalists "reported" that a local teenager was a suspect in the bombing, posting a photo of the boy standing in the crowd at the marathon. Internet users quickly identified the teenager. They began propagating[6] the rumor that he was being sought by the authorities, pulling photos from his Facebook page and circulating them widely. The *New York Post* picked up the story, even publishing the teenager's picture on its front page as the prime suspect in a murderous terrorist act. That same day, the newspaper was forced to retract[7] the story—authorities confirmed that the young man was entirely innocent. And while the *Post* apologized for not verifying its facts, none of the amateur investigative journalists ever did.

> **Q** What false rumor was spread by citizen journalists after the Boston bombing?

Crowdsourcing has become an invaluable tool for professional journalists and is not going away anytime soon. But stories like this one raise questions about journalistic standards. In the future, will citizen reporters create informed citizens or misinformed mobs[8]?

Online citizen journalists sometimes become cyber-bullies.

5	**aftermath**	*n.* the period of time after a bad and usually destructive event
6	**propagate**	*v.* to make known to many people
7	**retract**	*v.* to say that something you said or wrote is not true or correct
8	**mob**	*n.* a large crowd of people who are very angry or difficult to control

READING COMPREHENSION

A **Mark each statement as true (*T*) or false (*F*) according to the reading.**

1 ______ Rodney King was the first famous citizen journalist.

2 ______ Some news organizations encourage public participation.

3 ______ Many prominent journalists are skeptical of citizen journalism.

4 ______ The bombers in Boston were captured immediately.

5 ______ The *New York Post* repeated false information reported by citizen journalists.

B **Choose the best answer according to the reading.**

1 What is the main idea of the reading?

a. Citizen journalism is now part of the news process but has both pros and cons.
b. Citizen journalists are destroying the integrity of the news-gathering profession.
c. Professional journalists hypocritically insult citizen journalists while using their work.
d. Citizen journalism has overcome corporate-owned media and democratized the news.

2 The word these in paragraph 3 refers to ______.

a. images b. platforms
c. contributors d. organizations

3 We can guess from paragraphs 5 and 6 that citizen journalists ______.

a. should never try to report on terrorism
b. are always driven by fear and anger
c. should be more careful about fact-checking
d. have improved a lot since 2013

4 Which is NOT true about the *New York Post*?

a. It started the rumor that the teenager was a suspect.
b. It put the teenager's photo on its front page.
c. It admitted that the story about the teenager was false.
d. It apologized for getting the facts wrong.

SUMMARY

Fill in the blanks with the phrases in the box.

mobile devices	the Middle East	the news cycle
reporting and analysis	amateur journalists	participate directly

We are currently witnessing the rise of citizen journalism—an era in which regular people are participating in the news we watch. Citizen journalism means amateurs taking part in ❶ ________________. Photos and videos have been the most successful contributions, in large part because there are so many ❷ ________________ now—regular news teams simply cannot keep up. Rather than fight the trend, many news organizations search for public content or even invite the public to ❸ ________________. Some news events, like conflicts in ❹ ________________, could not have been covered as effectively without regular people contributing. But not everyone is enthusiastic about the trend, especially when it comes to ❺ ________________. Critics point out only professional journalists are trained and held accountable for the integrity of their work. And there are examples of ❻ ________________ making major mistakes, such as in their reporting about the Boston bombing.

DISCUSSION

Discuss the following questions with your partner or classmates.

1. How often do you watch amateur news-related videos?
2. Can you think of any recent events that citizen journalists helped to cover? Do you think this is a good idea? Explain.

WRITING

Write a short paragraph answering the following questions.

1. **What is a recent event that citizen journalists helped to cover? Why was their participation key to reporting this story?**
2. **What opinions accompanied the citizen reports? Do you think the citizens' opinions may have colored their reporting on the topic?**
3. **Do you think that professional reporters have motives other than a desire to inform the public about current events (e.g., political bias)?**

Example

Both citizen journalists and professional journalists have a role to play in the modern world. Citizen journalists help gather the news, while professional journalists work to interpret it. I think that both have a place, as long as they are both responsible in obtaining their information. If a citizen reporter isn't careful or responsible, the professionals should not use him or her as a source. This would work to maintain the media's credibility.

My Paragraph

Unit 3 • Careers

Reading 1 They Don't Live for Work ... They Work to Live

BEFORE YOU READ

Talk about these questions with your classmates.

The newest generation of job seekers differs from previous generations in certain ways. Think of at least two ways and discuss them with a partner.

Think About It

Do today's young workers make good employees?

VOCABULARY PREVIEW

Choose the one that is closest to the meaning of the word in bold.

1 Young people today don't have the same **conception** of work as their parents.
a. value b. skill c. idea

2 Generation Y employees care less about **compensation** and more about meaning.
a. status b. achievement c. pay

3 Young workers these days **prioritize** fulfillment and fun, regarding money and status as less important.
a. care most about b. greatly appreciate c. do not expect

4 Taking time off to travel is now the **norm**.
a. reward b. goal c. usual

5 James **convinced** the head of the company that he wasn't being rude.
a. informed b. persuaded c. reminded

They Don't Live for Work . . . They Work to Live

05

by Anushka Asthana © 2008, The Guardian News and Media Ltd. Used by permission.

Settling down on the shiny black sofa in the front room of their student house in Newcastle, Ailsa McNeil and her roommates discuss what they will do once they leave university.

"The idea of moving into the financial world of London and working long hours inside a massive company does not appeal to me," said McNeil.

Q What does Ailsa McNeil have in common with many other members of Generation Y?

She is not alone. New research has found that a similar attitude to work is widespread among the group of people known as Generation Y, usually defined as those born between the late 1980s and the year 2000. A study of more than 2,500 people in this group found that they were rejecting their parents' **conception** of work and were determined not to lead lives that revolved so heavily around their jobs.

Instead, they were ready to resign[1] if their work was not fulfilling and fun with a decent number of holidays and the opportunity to take long stretches off for charity work or travel. **Compensation** and status were not **prioritized,** according to the study by Talentsmoothie, a firm that advises companies on the changing workforce.

Today's young job seekers expect to get time off for travel.

The research concluded that this generation has "many choices: gap years[2] and extensive travel are the **norm**. They have seen their parents in stressful jobs working long hours and realize that hard work for big companies apparently does not bring prosperity[3] and happiness. . . . They want their lives to be different, and this shows. If they are dissatisfied, they resign."

C Underline the statistics in this paragraph. Find the sample size noted earlier in the passage, and circle it.

The study found that 85 percent of Generation Y wanted to spend 30 percent to 70 percent of their time working from home. More than half wanted a flexible working arrangement. The top priority when choosing a job was "doing work that I love," while "earning lots of money" was far behind, in seventh place.

That is why major companies, hoping to attract the very best graduates, are doing whatever they can to lure them in. "The previous generation saw work as a primary part of life," says Madalyn Brooks, HR director at Procter and Gamble. "Now, we are seeing the growth of a different profile[4] of candidates. They have grown up in relatively affluent

1 **resign** *v.* to quit a job or position
2 **gap year** *n.* a year off from school or work, often to travel
3 **prosperity** *n.* success; wealth
4 **profile** *n.* a list of characteristics that help identify someone

families. They want to be sure that they can strike a balance between work and their personal life, and so the opportunity to take time off, to travel, to work for a company with a strong social responsibility record—these are all concerns that we increasingly hear when recruiting talent."

Procter and Gamble has already adapted its recruitment efforts and what it offers to meet the needs of Generation Y. Instead of just stressing higher salaries, this company is highlighting the opportunity for flexible hours, the chance to work from home, and other perks[5]. Similar packages are being offered by companies across Britain.

Q How are companies adjusting to the new generation of workers?

However, the overconfidence of Generation Y is proving a challenge for employers. In fact, the research found that younger workers were far more willing to challenge managers and relatively unconcerned with hierarchy. In one case, outlined in the study, a chief executive of a large insurance firm emailed employees to inform them about a major decision. James, 24, who had recently joined the firm, told his older colleagues he disagreed with what had been done. He quickly decided to share his feelings with the head of the company and sent his thoughts directly to him in an email. A reply popped up on James's screen: "I have been running this company for ten years; I think I know what I am doing." James hit back: "I realize this is an uncomfortable conversation, but I am not the only one that disagrees with you." Luckily, he was able to **convince** the boss that he was not simply being rude.

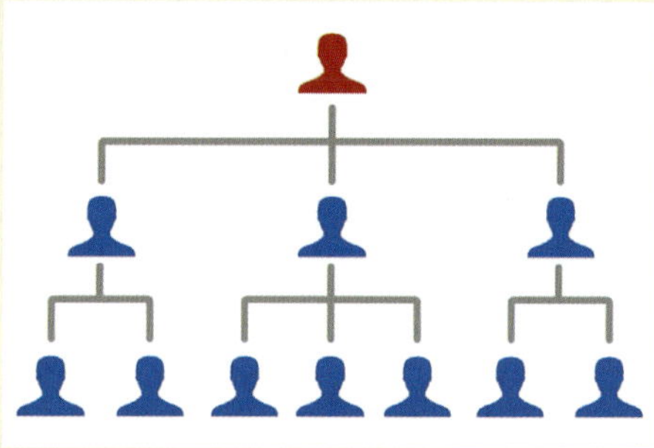

Young people pay less attention to company hierarchies than previous generations did.

Simon Walker, a founding director of Talentsmoothie, said he planned to look at how attitudes differed across the world. He argued that they were partly dictated[6] by age but also by circumstances. In China, Generation Y is made up of only-children, as a result of the one-child policy, who grew up through difficult economic times. They would have very different values from their British counterparts, he said.

Q What are two factors that affect people's attitudes toward employment according to Simon Walker? Circle them.

In Britain, meanwhile, there would be people of all ages who shared typical Generation Y attitudes, he argued, but they would be far more common within the age group. One of those attitudes, according to research by Walker and others, is a strong desire to be fulfilled in their jobs.

"We see young people that are searching for some sort of meaning in life," said Julia Middleton, the group's chief executive. "I think life is cyclical, and there is a return to people searching for meaning and searching for values."

5 **perk** *n.* something an employee gets in addition to pay

6 **dictate** *v.* to determine; to require

READING COMPREHENSION

A **Organize the ideas from the reading. Review the passage and fill in the graphic organizer below.**

Generation Y and their conception of work

Have different view of work:	Cause companies to change policies to attract them:	Place less importance on
• Saw parents work stressful jobs • Care less about salary, more about [1] ____________ • Willing to resign if [2] ____________	e.g.: Procter and Gamble offering [3] ____________ ____________	[4] ____________: e.g.: 24-year-old James criticized [5] ____________ ____________

Want meaningful work and a good work-life balance

B **Choose the best answer according to the reading.**

1 What can be inferred about Generation Y from paragraph 5?

a. Few of them have parents who worked for big companies.
b. Many do not think their parents found fulfillment in their work.
c. Their parents have advised them not to care too much about salary.
d. Most still depend on their parents for money.

2 According to paragraph 9, which of the following is true?

a. James was an experienced employee when that incident happened.
b. James's older colleagues told him to send the boss a message.
c. James told his boss in an email that he disagreed with him.
d. James's boss replied by thanking James for his input.

SUMMARY

Fill in the blanks with the phrases in the box.

personal fulfillment	across cultures	different attitude
work from home	high salaries	these perks

Research shows that members of Generation Y have a ❶ _______________ toward work than their parents. These young people, born between the late 1980s and 2000, value ❷ _______________ and free time more than ❸ _______________ and status. Most of them also want flexible work arrangements with opportunities to ❹ _______________. Companies such as Procter and Gamble are trying to attract young workers by offering ❺ _______________. However, some employers find the overconfidence of Generation Y challenging. For example, these young employees are more willing to criticize their bosses. Research also suggests that attitudes among members of Generation Y may differ ❻ _______________.

DISCUSSION

A Read the excerpt from the reading passage.

They Don't Live for Work . . . They Work to Live

Simon Walker, a founding director of Talentsmoothie, said he planned to look at how attitudes differed across the world. He argued that they were partly dictated by age but also by circumstances. In China, Generation Y is made up of only-children, as a result of the one-child policy, who grew up through difficult economic times. They would have very different values to their British counterparts, he said.

B Discuss the following questions with your partner or classmates.

1. How do you think values among young people in China might differ from those in Britain?
2. Do you think your country's Generation Y is similar to that of Britain? Why or why not?
3. What disadvantages could there be to the Generation Y values described in the article?

WRITING

Write a short paragraph answering the following question.

Q: In general, do you think members of Generation Y make good employees?

☐ **[Opinion 1]** Yes, I think members of Generation Y make good employees.

☐ **[Opinion 2]** No, I do not think members of Generation Y make good employees.

Example

I think members of Generation Y make good employees. First, they are the most technologically advanced generation in history. This is the first generation to have been born during the Internet Age. Computer skills will only increase in importance in the future economy. Second, millennials don't care much about hierarchy, which can lead to innovation and positive change. Junior employees often have great, original ideas. It's good that young people today are not afraid to speak out in front of their bosses. Third, young people today seek meaning in what they do. Research shows that most Millennials are not motivated mainly by money but by fulfillment. If you give them meaningful goals, they will pursue those goals with enthusiasm. Some employers think Millennials have bad attitudes. This is how every generation sees the later one. The older generation will have to accept that this is the new way of thinking. In short, millennials are certain to have a positive impact on the workplace by bringing to it new ways of thinking about work and life.

My Paragraph

Reading 2 Breaking Free of 9 to 5

BEFORE YOU READ

Talk about these questions with your classmates.

This passage is an article about the usual 9 to 5 workday. What is one advantage of having everyone in a company work the same hours in the same place? What is one disadvantage?

Think About It

What can companies do to make working conditions better for employees?

VOCABULARY PREVIEW

Choose the one that is closest to the meaning of the word in bold.

1 Some people are most **energetic** in the morning.
a. cheerful b. active c. relaxed

2 The reasons for adopting the forty-hour workweek might **justify** not getting rid of it.
a. cause to end b. make necessary c. provide a good reason for

3 Henry Ford **instituted** a five-day workweek in his factories.
a. invented b. established c. rejected

4 Gradually, governments started to **legislate** working hours.
a. put into law b. research c. have debates about

5 An eight-hour workday became the **convention** in the business world.
a. custom b. goal c. strategy

Breaking Free of 9 to 5

06

by Jim Edwards

When we started our own company, my partners and I just assumed that we'd keep regular office hours. Every other job any of us had ever had was like that. Why would ours be any different?

However, it quickly became clear that things weren't going to play out[1] that way. The thing is that, like many developers, I'm a night owl[2]. I don't get going until about noon, and I'm at my most productive[3] between 8 p.m. and midnight. My co-founders are the complete opposite; they're most **energetic** first thing in the morning, and by mid-afternoon, they're ready to crash. For the first three months, we all struggled—I with the morning meetings, they with my late-night phone calls. Forcing everyone to work on the same schedule quickly proved to be an exercise in frustration. We just weren't being as productive as we could be, and we all knew it.

Q How is the author different from his co-founders?

The problems our fledgling[4] startup faced made us examine our assumptions about our working hours. Why do most people work a 9-to-5 day, five days a week? A quick look at the history of working hours reveals just how outdated our current standard is.

That Was Then, This Is Now

The current workday emerged almost a hundred years ago, in a different era. However, if there were good reasons for it—reasons that still apply today—then perhaps that could **justify** not abandoning it.

Well, the fact is that there were never very convincing reasons for adopting the forty-hour workweek. During the 1920s, the Industrial Revolution was in full swing. Factories typically ran twenty-four hours a day, with workers putting in ten- to sixteen-hour shifts. Then, Ford Motor Company founder Henry Ford **instituted** a five-day, forty-hour workweek in his factories but still paid his workers the same wages. Surprisingly, it wasn't his intention to improve his workers' quality of life, their health, or even their productivity. Ford later explained in interviews that he had made the change to a forty-hour workweek to give workers more time to shop—specifically, to buy his cars. Regardless of the motivation, other manufacturers followed suit[5] and more workers started demanding the same conditions. Gradually, governments started **legislating** the forty-hour workweek as part of labor law. The 9-to-5 workday soon became the **convention** in almost all industries.

Q What change did Henry Ford make? Why did he make it?

You no longer have to be in the office to be productive.

At the time, a uniform work schedule for everyone did make some sense. After all, the office was the locus[6] of work, and workers had to be available during work hours to collaborate[7] in person. There were no other options. However, in the era of laptops, cell phones, ubiquitous[8] wireless connectivity, and cloud solutions, do arguments for this model really carry any weight? If workers can work from anywhere at any time, why

---

1 **play out** *phrasal v.* to develop; to become in the end
2 **night owl** *n.* a person who likes to stay up late
3 **productive** *adj.* working hard and getting a lot done
4 **fledgling** *adj.* newly formed and still developing
5 **follow suit** *idiom* to do the same as
6 **locus** *n.* a central place; a site where something happens
7 **collaborate** *v.* to work together on something
8 **ubiquitous** *adj.* found everywhere; very common

should they have to come in to the office at 9 and leave at 5? Beyond the occasional face-to-face meeting, there seems to be no justification for having all workers follow the same schedule. The forty-hour workweek definitely seems outdated.

Night Owls in an Early-Bird World

The conventional workday is ideal for one type of person in particular: the early bird[9]. Research shows that genetic factors determine the length of a person's circadian cycle, the series of biochemical signals that influence the body's rise and fall in energy levels and trigger drowsiness, wakefulness, hunger, etc. This cycle determines whether someone is an early bird or a night owl, according to Katherine Sharkey, a professor at Brown University and the associate director of the Sleep for Science Research Lab. If your cycle is a bit shorter, you're most likely an early bird and the 9-to-5 routine suits you just fine. When you come in to work in the morning, you're all fired up and ready to go; and by the end of the day, your energy level starts to drop off.

C Circle the term that is defined in this paragraph. Underline the definition.

But what if, like a sizable[10] proportion of the population, you are more productive later in the day or even at night? The 9-to-5 routine forces night owls to try to be productive at times when their alertness and energy level are lowest. As a result, night owls typically get a reputation for being lazy or unmotivated. This is unfair, given that they are merely victims of their own wake-sleep cycle, which they are more or less incapable of changing. However, if given the chance to work on a schedule that better suits them, night owls can be just as productive as early birds and may actually outperform[11] them.

C Summarize the argument in this paragraph.

Breaking from Tradition

When my co-founders and I sat down to re-evaluate our approach to working hours, the change was an easy sell. But the mental shift to the new approach didn't come naturally. Even now, three years later, I still find myself checking the time periodically[12] through the day, particularly in the late afternoon, and calculating how many more hours I should put in. On days when I work less than eight hours, I have to admit that I still feel a bit guilty—like I'm not working as hard as I could or that I'm cheating someone. But on another level, I'm well aware that this way of thinking is wrong.

Several steps led to our company's eventual break from the traditional 9-to-5 schedule. Originally, we adopted a flextime system. Everyone had to be at the office between 11 a.m. and 3 p.m., beyond which they could just come and go as they liked, provided they worked a full eight hours a day. However, flextime was abandoned after a few months, too. The quantitative measure of how many hours someone worked just wasn't as important to us as the qualitative aspect. We wanted beautiful, creative products and brilliant solutions to problems, and we found we got more of those out of our team when we let them set their own schedules.

Q Why did the company eventually abandon flextime? Underline the information.

Now our work schedules are guided by our energy levels and the specific projects we have to get done. Instead of forcing ourselves to be productive at certain times, we can all customize our schedule to ideally suit our individual lifestyles. We care not about how many hours we work, but about what we do in those hours.

On the surface, having no set working hours might seem like a recipe for disaster, but for our company it's been perfect. Since abandoning a set work schedule, we've seen improvements in our productivity, the quality of our work, our health, and the overall quality of our lives. It's a decision we've never regretted, and it's one I would recommend other business owners give some serious thought to.

---

9 **early bird** *n.* a person who likes to get up early
10 **sizable** *adj.* fairly large
11 **outperform** *v.* to perform better than
12 **periodically** *adv.* from time to time

READING COMPREHENSION

A **Organize the ideas from the reading. Review the passage and fill in the graphic organizer below.**

Breaking free of the 9-to-5 workday

History:

1920s, Industrial Revolution: people worked 1 ______________

Forty-hour workweek: started by Henry Ford; became the 2 ______________

Made sense before Internet

Why it should change:

Cell phones and Internet allow people to work anywhere, anytime

Circadian cycle: genetically determined

3 ______________ not productive in the morning

After the change:

4 ______________ to make the mental shift

Work guided by energy levels; quality more important than quantity

Improvements in 5 ______________

No regrets about the decision

B **Choose the best answer according to the reading.**

1 What is the main idea of paragraph 6?

a. Technology allows people to do their jobs wherever they want.
b. Changes in technology have removed the need for a 9-to-5 workday.
c. Nowadays, it is rare for all the workers in an office to have the same schedule.
d. Cell phones and computers mean people no longer communicate face-to-face.

2 What can be inferred about the author and his co-workers from paragraphs 10-11?

a. They all have fairly similar habits and lifestyles.
b. They are working fewer hours per week than before.
c. They are having trouble adjusting to the new system.
d. They work more hours on some days than on others.

SUMMARY

Fill in the blanks with the phrases in the box.

energy levels	more productive	have improved
seem outdated	number of hours	early birds

The Early Days of the Company	• The partners kept regular office hours. • This caused frustration because one partner was ❶ __________ in the evenings than in the mornings.
Why They Changed	• The 9-to-5, five-day workweek made more sense in the past, when the office or factory was the locus of work (e.g., the Ford Motor Company). • Technology that allows co-workers to communicate has caused this model to ❷ __________. • Some people are night owls, and others are ❸ __________, for biological reasons. • Flextime was tried but abandoned because it still relied on counting the ❹ __________ worked.
The Results	• Now the partners' schedules are guided by their ❺ __________ and project goals, and are adapted to each individual. • Their productivity, work quality, and overall well-being ❻ __________.

DISCUSSION

A Read the excerpt from the reading passage.

Breaking Free of 9 to 5

Now our work schedules are guided by our energy levels and the specific projects we have to get done. Instead of forcing ourselves to be productive at certain times, we can all customize our schedule to ideally suit our individual lifestyles. We care not about how many hours we work, but about what we do in those hours.

B Discuss the following questions with your partner or classmates.

1 Why might some people think this system seems like "a recipe for disaster," as the author puts it?

2 Think of the type of job you have or intend to have someday. Would a customized schedule like this be possible and effective for you? Why or why not?

WRITING

Write a short paragraph answering the following question.

Q: What should today's employers do to make sure their employees are productive and happy?

☐ **[Opinion]** To make employees happy and productive, I think employers should allow flexible schedules, ____________________, and ____________________.

Example

To make employees happy and productive, I think employers should allow flexible schedules, provide the opportunity to telecommute, and offer plenty of benefits. Employers should allow flexible schedules. Different people are productive at different times of day. Unlike early birds, night owls work best late in the day, so they will accomplish more if allowed a different work schedule. Employers should offer the chance to telecommute. Working from home saves time and money on commuting. It also benefits people who work best when they're alone, without noise and interruptions. Companies should provide plenty of benefits. Google, for example, offers health care on site, a gym, and even free haircuts. These things provide employees convenience and make them feel valued, thereby raising productivity and loyalty. You might think that money is the most important thing a company can offer. However, having more money does not always result in a better quality of life, which should be the ultimate goal of making money. Following the above recommendations will help companies promote productivity and loyalty among employees.

My Paragraph

Unit 4 • Engineering

Reading 1 Five Routes to the Future

BEFORE YOU READ

Talk about these questions with your classmates.

Many modern cities have convenient facilities for residents that are designed to reduce society's negative effects on the environment. What are some examples that you know? Write a list and share it with a partner.

VOCABULARY PREVIEW

Match each word in bold with its meaning in the box.

a. creative and new	b. capable of continuing for a long time
c basic structure underlying a concept	d. the building process e. the act of using up

_____ **1** For a community to be **sustainable**, it must balance human needs with the environment.

_____ **2** Urban planners created a **framework** to guide the city's development project.

_____ **3** The city developed **innovative** policies to protect the environment.

_____ **4** **Construction** of the light railway system took the environment into consideration.

_____ **5** People can use the technology to measure their daily energy **consumption**.

Five Routes to the Future 07

by Kate Morris

Q What is the main point of the passage? Underline it.

At first glance[1], a multimillion dollar property development in South Korea does not have much in common with one of Europe's oldest settlements. But what unites Songdo and Nice, along with the three other cities featured here, is a willingness to take on new ideas and a bold approach to implementing them. Nice, Medellín Songdo, Portland, and Coventry have a particular vision of becoming world leaders in urban planning and models for cutting carbon emissions[2]. And they are going about it in a "smart" way.

Songdo, South Korea

Central Park in Songdo is South Korea's model for green cities.

Imagine a city with no traffic jams, where air conditioning, heating, and lights can be controlled from a mobile phone or computer. Video-conferencing screens in every apartment and "green meters" allow residents to track their daily energy **consumption**.

This is smart life in Songdo, South Korea, the private $35 million (£21.5 million) development founded in August 2009 on a man-made island in the Yellow Sea. It is expected to have a population of 65,000 and up to 300,000 daily commuters[3].

Forty percent of Songdo is green space, including a 100-acre park at the heart of the city. Water taxis are already navigating the city's seawater canal[4] system, and a bicycle rental system is to start next year on the city's 25 kilometers of bicycle lanes.

All offices, retail shops, and homes are constructed to strict environmental standards. While a network of pipes removes solid waste, used city water and rain are collected for irrigation[5] and are recycled.

Q What is Songdo's solution to traffic problems?

And how will they stop traffic jams? Controllers will track people as they make journeys across the city and, by studying previous trips, will trigger the traffic lights as needed.

Portland, US

Portland, home to around 500,000 people in the north-western US, is leading the way in smart and **innovative** environmental legislation. It also ranks in the top ten green cities in the world. "We find when you focus on helping people live an easier, more robust[6] life, the environment wins, too," says Susan Anderson, the director of the city's department of planning and sustainability.

Q What role did the Portland community play in the construction of the light railway system?

The resolve of its residents to lead a more environmentally smart lifestyle dates back to the 1970s. At that time, community-led protests forced a switch of public money from a new freeway to a light railway system. Opened in 1986, the 52-mile railway is now hailed[7] as a model of environmentally friendly **construction** practices.

---

1. **glance** *n.* a quick look
2. **carbon emissions** *n.* gases that are released when burning fossil fuels like oil or coal
3. **commuter** *n.* a person who travels regularly between two points, usually home and workplace
4. **canal** *n.* a man-made channel of water used by boats or to carry water to crops
5. **irrigation** *n.* the act of supplying water to land or crops
6. **robust** *adj.* strong, healthy, and full of energy
7. **hail** *v.* to give enthusiastic approval or praise for someone or something

In 1993, Portland became the first US local authority[8] to adopt a plan to reduce climate change. By 2009, total carbon dioxide emissions in the region were two percent below 1990 national levels and fifteen percent below 2000 levels, despite rapid growth of the city.

Last year, the city signed on to the EV (electric vehicle) Project, the largest such plan in the world, according to Ecotality, the company behind it. An initial thirty-six charging stations in the city will grow to five hundred by next year.

Coventry, UK

This summer, Coventry, in the West Midlands, hit on a new mode of using technology to gather the opinions of its residents. Partnering with IBM, it held a three-day mass online conversation—called CovJam, between some 3,000 residents, politicians, and council officers. The ideas that emerged from this discussion are now being used to reshape the authority's **sustainable** communities strategy.

Becoming the first UK local authority to launch such an online session demonstrates the council's desire to "take risks and innovate." It also reflects the city's position as a high-tech center with local science parks and two universities—Warwick and Coventry—that specialize in advanced research.

A long-time supporter of alternative sources of energy, the city council bought its first electric vehicle back in 1995. Coventry is also one of only six UK authorities signed on to the government's Low-Carbon Vehicle Procurement Programme. Now the city has forty-five low-carbon vehicles for various public service tasks.

Q What environmental technology do the cities of Portland and Coventry have in common?

Another local business, Microcab, is making cars powered by hydrogen. The city also boasts[9] eighteen electric charging stations and a hydrogen refueling station, one of only a handful in the country.

Medellín, Colombia

Medellíns £44.5 million cable car system carrying those living in the sprawling barrios above the city to its center is more than just an integrated transport project.

The cable cars are at the centre of a unique social and urban development **framework** that has helped reduce the Colombian city's high murder rate. This demonstrates how "smart" projects can help solve social issues.

It was led by the city's then mayor Sergio Fajardo and a team of experts in various fields, who believed integrating the city's poor was central to reducing gang violence.

The first cable cars started running in 2004, offering residents in the barrio of Santo Domingo a seven-minute ride to the centre of Medellín. This dramatically shortened their journey, which previously took one or two hours by minibus.

Over the following four years, a second line was constructed. In addition, libraries and child-care facilities have been built in and around the cable car stations in the distant towns.

C Medellín's new urban design is said to result in decreased crime. What evidence is used to prove this?

While crime remains a problem in Medellín, the murder rate has more than halved from 3,557 in 2002 to 1,717 last year.

Nice, France

Nice has become the first European city to use near-field communication (NFC) technology to permit payment at public places. People in Nice can now make purchases at shops, museums, and galleries, as well as on trams and buses, via smart phones. The ultimate goal is to end the use of paper or plastic money to pay for various local goods and services.

---

[8] **authority** *n.* a person or institution that has the power or control in a situation

[9] **boast** *v.* to have, or feature, something positive

At the moment, only Samsung phones, available from four local networks, have the NFC chip. But the hope is that eventually it will be on all new mobiles. Also, fifteen more French cities are considering following Nice's example.

Christian Estrosi, the mayor of Nice and minister for industry in the French government, says he believes strongly in making the city an area where innovation can grow. "Innovation improves the well-being of our people, as well as triggering growth and jobs for the future."

Reading 1

READING COMPREHENSION

A Organize the ideas from the reading. Review the passage and fill in the graphic organizer below.

Green cities of the future

Songdo
- Use [1] ________________ on the city's waterways
- Collect and [2] ________________ rain and waste water

Portland
- In the top ten [3] ________________ worldwide
- Promote use of [4] ________________ for vehicles

[5] ________________
- High-tech center with science parks and universities
- Has one of a few [6] ________________ in UK

Medellín
- Serve barrios with ________ system
- Built ________ and child-care facilities

Nice
- Enable ________ technology for purchases
- Replace ________ money for payments

B Choose the best answer according to the reading.

1 What did the cable car system do for Santo Domingo in Colombia?

a. It reduced carbon emissions because fewer people now drive cars.
b. It cut down the commuting time to Medellín to seven minutes.
c. It was the main reason for Mayor Sergio Fajardo's re-election.
d. It increased the city's revenue by tens of millions of pounds.

2 Where did the ideas come from for reshaping Coventry's sustainable communities strategy?

a. A committee of experts in consultation with the mayor
b. A study of models that worked in other cities
c. A survey of customers at local restaurants and shops
d. An online discussion that involved various community members

SUMMARY

Fill in the blanks with the phrases in the box.

charging stations	online conversation	cable-car system
environmental standards	by smart phone	man-made island

Songdo	Portland	Coventry	Medellín	Nice
• A private development on a(n) ❶ ________ • Forty-percent green space • All buildings follow strict ❷ ________	• Environmentally friendly light-rail system • Hundreds of ❸ ________ for EVs	• Held a mass ❹ ________ to gather opinions and ideas • Owns 45 low-carbon vehicles; produces hydrogen-powered cars	• Built a(n) ❺ ________ to integrate the poor and reduce the murder rate • Built libraries and child-care facilities	• First European city to adopt NFC • Payment ❻ ________ reduces use of paper or plastic money

DISCUSSION

Ⓐ Read the excerpt from the reading passage.

Five Routes to the Future

But what unites Songdo and Nice, along with the three other cities featured here, is a willingness to take on new ideas and a bold approach to implementing them. Nice, Medellín, Songdo, Portland, and Coventry have a particular vision of becoming world leaders in urban planning and models for cutting carbon emissions.

Ⓑ Discuss the following questions with your partner or classmates.

1 Which of the innovations described in the passage have you heard of before? Which have you not heard of before?

2 Which of the cities would you like to live in? Why?

WRITING

Write a short paragraph answering the following question.

Q: What are some changes you'd like to see made to your city?

☐ **[Opinion]** If I were an urban planner for my city, there are various changes that I would make, including building a light railway system, ________________, and ________________.

Example

If I were an urban planner for my city, there are various changes that I would make, including building a light railway system, creating more green spaces, and replacing government vehicles with those powered by renewable energy. Improving public transportation is one of the best ways to develop a city. Not only does it help the environment by giving people an alternative to driving, it also helps those who cannot afford their own transportation. Incorporating more greenery within interior and exterior designs will make the living environment more pleasant. I am especially interested in setting up living walls inside buildings and increasing the number of natural areas around the city because they will lead to improved working and learning environments for all local residents. Replacing all gas engine vehicles used by the government with more environmentally friendly models will make a big difference in efforts to protect the environment. Opponents would argue that these urban projects will cost the city too much money, time, and effort. My response is that the great benefits to the community and the environment are well worth the price. With these reasons in mind, I urge city officials to seriously consider my recommendations.

My Paragraph

Unit 4 • Engineering

Reading 2 Drive My Car ... Please

BEFORE YOU READ

Talk about these questions with your classmates.

We may soon see self-driving vehicles on our roads. What advantages might these vehicles have over traditional cars? Think of two ideas and discuss them with a partner.

Think About It

What technology might have the greatest impact on society in the future?

VOCABULARY PREVIEW

Match each word in bold with its meaning in the box.

a. as a result
b. to guess what will happen and prepare
c. to admit
d. a typical example or pattern of something; a model
e. early; at the beginning

_____ **1** Traffic accidents will decrease, and **consequently** the number of traffic deaths will drop.

_____ **2** The writer **acknowledges** that self-driving cars are likely to be on the road in the future.

_____ **3** The cars can **anticipate** braking and accelerating, so they will use less gas.

_____ **4** **Preliminary** estimates suggest that self-driving cars would save many lives each year.

_____ **5** Self-driving cars are an entirely new automotive **paradigm**.

Drive My Car . . . Please

08

by Jon Maes / Language Cradle Consulting

C Why does the author quote Donald Blaise?

Normally, I'm 100 percent supportive of the acclaimed[1] columnist Donald Blaise's innovative and sometimes unusual ideas. But reading his recent article "Just Say 'No' to Self-driving Cars," I was surprised by his argument against this exciting new technology. How could a champion[2] of new ideas be against self-driving cars? Though he **acknowledges** that their use in the future is very likely, he goes on to write: "Self-driving cars are a terrible idea because a human being has no control over the vehicle!"

Well, Donald, that's kind of the point, don't you think? Self-driving cars are actually a fantastic idea because they will do exactly what the name implies—they'll handle the driving for you! When the car takes control, the driver will be safer, freer, and happier. Blaise's explanation for why self-driving cars are terrible is exactly why they're so amazing.

C Besides statistics, what does the author use to support his opinion about self-driving cars?
(1) Personal experience
(2) Research findings
(3) Expert opinion

Self-driving cars could help prevent this.

Mr. Blaise, as it turns out, does most of his work from home. He doesn't have to sit in his car every morning and afternoon, moving slowly along a busy highway bumper-to-bumper with his fellow commuters. If there is even one fender-bender[3] along my route to work, I can be delayed up to an hour. Perhaps Blaise didn't happen to read the recent study by the National Highway Traffic Safety Administration which found that self-driving cars could reduce traffic congestion by more than seventy-five percent. The computers driving the cars will be able to communicate and basically choreograph[4] their own dance, moving around one another without having to slow down to a crawl. The technology would allow cars to check in with each other, anticipate[5] their movements, and work around them.

Q Why does the author think that computers make better drivers than humans do? Underline at least three things.

Computers just do some things better than people do—and more importantly, they can perform several tasks concurrently. They can't be distracted by birds, billboards, or loud motorcycles. They also can't drink, take drugs, or get tired. Ninety percent of all vehicular accidents are caused by the drivers' own errors. A computer, however, is far less likely to make any kind of slip-up[6] that might result from such mistakes. Once human error is taken out of the equation, traffic accidents—and **consequently**, deaths and injuries—plummet[7].

One of Blaise's complaints about self-driving cars was that the technology would be too expensive. He claimed that only a small percentage of the general population would be able to afford it, making any positive impacts too small to be worth the expense. But **preliminary** estimates by the non-profit group Eno Center for Transportation predict that if only ten percent of the vehicles on the road were self-driving, 1,100 lives could

1 **acclaimed** *adj.* popular and respected
2 **champion (of something)** *n.* a promoter or advocate of something
3 **fender-bender** *n.* a minor car accident
4 **choreograph** *v.* to design or arrange the movements of a dance
5 **anticipate** *v.* to expect what could happen in the future and prepare for it
6 **slip-up** *n.* a mistake
7 **plummet** *v.* to decrease rapidly

Self-driving cars could also prevent this from happening so often.

be saved a year in the US alone. Forget about cutting my morning commute to the office down by a few minutes—this technology could actually save lives.

Q What might happen if one out of ten cars on the road were self-driving? Underline the information.

Like most technologies, self-driving cars will, of course, be expensive. The cost of the software, sensors, and power alone for one of these cars could well exceed $100,000 per vehicle. But Blaise's weak argument against the cost will soon become irrelevant. As with any technology, the cost will eventually go down. In the early 1970s, a personal home computer could cost tens of thousands of dollars, but today you can buy a slim, stylish laptop for only a few hundred dollars. There's no reason to assume that the cost of self-driving cars wouldn't go the same way.

C What analogy does the author use to support his prediction that self-driving cars will eventually become affordable?

As the cost of self-driving cars goes down, the benefits will only continue to increase. Once ninety percent of the cars on the road are self-driving, 4.2 billion accidents could be avoided, and 21,700 lives saved. And lives won't be the only thing being saved—when cars can **anticipate** braking and accelerating, they will use less gas, costing their owners less money and helping our ailing environment.

Do you know what else the self-driving car will save? Sanity[8]. How many poor drivers have ever cried out in frustration after their third attempt at trying to parallel park[9] their cars? The technology for a self-parking car is already out there. At the 2013 International Consumer Electronics Show, the Audi RS7 Sportback SUV gave an impressive performance, parking itself neatly into a spot while the driver stood on the curb, giving the vehicle commands from a smartphone app. No scratches. No bumps. No need to leave an awkward note on someone's windshield, apologizing for the new dent you gave his or her new convertible.

(A) With over 800,000 driverless miles logged[10] (and counting), Google is presently number one. (B) That's 800,000 miles without a single crash. (C) And Google isn't holding back on where their success comes from, either. (D) Their so-called "Chauffeur system" uses lidar—basically radar and sonar combined—which can take a million measurements per second to make a 3D model of the area you're driving in. It already knows where the stationary things are—crosswalks, telephone poles, and traffic lights—and then uses lidar to fill in the gaps with moving objects. It will see the neighbor's cat dashing[11] out into the road before you do. It will know that there's a bicyclist coming up behind you. It will sense all of the things that a distracted driver might overlook, and take the actions needed to prevent any accidents. At the moment, the Chauffeur costs around $75,000, but the geniuses at Google are already working to lower the price, hopefully moving into a more affordable range by 2018.

Q What sensing technologies does Google's driverless car use?

Donald doesn't have to drive to work. Maybe he can't imagine the bliss[12] that would come from climbing into his car with the morning paper, a hot mug of coffee, and a warm croissant. He doesn't know the joy that would come from sitting back and having a relaxing, easy, accident-free commute, arriving at work feeling relaxed and without any stress or anxiety. Maybe Donald is simply uncomfortable with this new automotive **paradigm**, but I'm not—I want it!

8 **sanity** *n.* the state of positive mental health
9 **parallel park** *v.* to park parallel to a curb, between two other cars
10 **log** *v.* to travel and record a certain distance
11 **dash** *v.* to run quickly
12 **bliss** *n.* complete happiness

READING COMPREHENSION

Choose the best answer according to the reading.

1 What can be inferred about author Donald Blaise?

a. He thinks that human drivers make too many errors.
b. He knows the author of "Drive My Car . . . Please" personally.
c. He prefers to remain in control of his own car.
d. He does not typically write about new technology.

2 Which of the following is NOT true according to the article?

a. Self-driving cars would result in seventy-five percent fewer traffic fatalities each year.
b. Self-driving cars could reduce traffic congestion by over half of its current level.
c. The computers in self-driving cars will actually communicate with those of other cars.
d. The operating systems in self-driving vehicles can do several things at once.

3 Which of the following does the author mention as being advantages of self-driving cars? (More than one answer is possible.)

a. Increased safety
b. Low starting costs
c. Higher economic output
d. Improved mental health of drivers
e. Greater energy efficiency

4 Where does the following sentence fit best in paragraph 9? Choose one of the letters (A) to (D).

> Audi isn't even the leader in this technology.

a. (A) b. (B) c. (C) d. (D)

5 Which of the following is true of lidar, according to paragraph 9?

a. It uses cameras to locate objects near the car.
b. Its first version will be developed by 2018.
c. Its price has already dropped significantly.
d. It can sense moving objects in all directions.

SUMMARY

Write the number of each sentence under the category it belongs to.

Self-driving Cars	
Complaints / Weak Points	Advantages

1. Self-driving cars easily perform tasks that are difficult for drivers, such as parallel parking.
2. The technology that makes self-driving cars possible is expensive.
3. According to one study, self-driving cars could reduce traffic congestion by over seventy-five percent.
4. Alcohol and drugs cannot affect the performance of self-driving cars.
5. There is no human being in control of a self-driving car.
6. Self-driving cars are safer and cannot be distracted by billboards or motorcycles.

DISCUSSION

Discuss the following questions with your partner or classmates.

1 Do you think people in your country would like self-driving cars? Explain your opinion.

2 Can you think of any drawbacks to self-driving vehicles?

WRITING

Write a short paragraph answering the following question.

Q: In your opinion, what new invention or technology will have the greatest impact on human beings?

☐ **[Opinion]** I think that advances in medical technology will transform human life more than any other technology will.

Example

I think that advances in medical technology will transform human life more than any other technology will. That's not to say that other technologies won't bring major changes. Advances in transportation, for instance, will very likely change the way people commute, travel, and get around in general. However, these changes won't affect humanity as much as medical advances will, one example being nanomedicine. For one thing, the medical application of nanotechnology will extend people's lives. Researchers are working on an exciting new way to treat cancer, by using tiny drug carriers to attack cancer cells specifically. This not only makes the treatment more effective but also reduces the severe side effects that accompany conventional chemotherapy. Besides extending human life, nanotechnology can improve it as well. Researchers are also using nanotechnology to treat people with serious backbone injuries by promoting the growth of new nerve fibers. Medical advances brought about by nanotechnology will have a great impact on human life, allowing people to live longer and improving the quality of life.

My Paragraph

Unit 5 • Law & Crime

Reading 1 Lie Detectors

BEFORE YOU READ

Talk about these questions with your classmates.

1 Are you good at guessing when other people are lying?
2 How does the body change when someone lies?
3 Have you ever been caught lying? What happened?

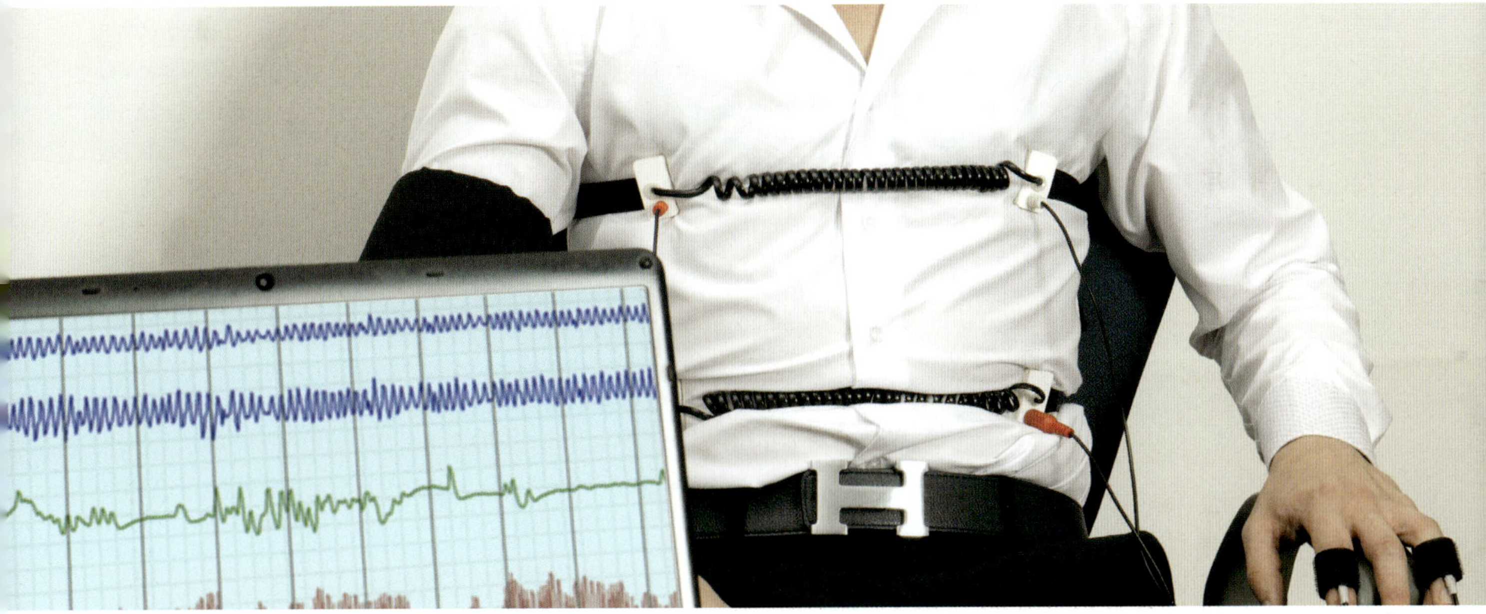

VOCABULARY PREVIEW

Fill in the blanks with the words in the box. Change the form of the word if necessary.

accurately	conduction	minimal	punish	reliability

1 There is an important difference between the prisoners who are dangerous and those we merely wish to ________________.

2 Insulation is used to keep buildings warm by preventing the ________________ of heat through the walls.

3 You can keep your room clean with ________________ effort if you pick things up regularly instead of putting it off until later.

4 Mom is practical: safety, gas mileage, and ________________ are the things she looks for in a car.

5 Standardized tests don't always ________________ predict success in higher education.

Lie Detectors 09

> **Q** Circle the two types of polygraph machines.

> **Q** What three signs of stress does a polygraph machine detect?

Polygraphs, or instruments used to discover whether a person is lying, are commonly called lie detectors. Polygraphs are utilized in courts, in the government, and in private businesses. However, they are controversial. Many people don't believe that polygraphs can **accurately** identify whether an individual is lying, while others believe that polygraphs are simply tools to intimidate[1] people into confessing guilt, regardless of whether they're really lying.

The older, analog polygraph machine consists of three styluses—or pens—and a roll of paper that slides across the machine. The styluses, which draw lines on the paper and record changes in the subject's condition, are connected to wires, which are in turn connected to the test subject. A mostly straight line indicates there is minimal variation in the subject's body. A jagged[2] line with multiple peaks and valleys illustrates a large amount of variation. Modern digital polygraphs are interpreted in a fashion identical[3] to analog polygraphs; however, instead of paper, the lines are displayed on a computer monitor.

Polygraph tests are interviews. Examiners ask subjects questions, and when subjects answer, their body reactions are recorded by the polygraph. During the interviews, examiners document the behavior of the lines on the paper subsequent to each question. Later, examiners use these results to assess the likelihood that the subject is telling the truth. When lying, individuals are often apprehensive[4] about being caught, and this uneasiness produces stress. Stress triggers elevated heart and breathing rates and an increase in perspiration[5], all of which are then detected by the polygraph.

To detect changes in respiration, rubber tubes filled with air are positioned around subjects' torsos, and as subjects breathe, air in the tubes is compressed[6] and the tubes expand. When the tubes expand, they push against a part of the polygraph called the bellows. The greater the expansion of the tubes, the greater the contraction of the bellows, which moves an arm on the polygraph. Breathing quickly results in an irregular line on the test. To measure heart rate, subjects wear bands around their wrists[7]. A tube connects the band to a second arm on the polygraph.

Lying has physical effects on most people.

1	**intimidate**	*v.* to fill with fear
2	**jagged**	*adj.* uneven; having sharp points
3	**identical**	*adj.* exactly the same
4	**apprehensive**	*adj.* nervous
5	**perspiration**	*n.* sweat
6	**compress**	*v.* to press or squeeze
7	**wrist**	*n.* the part of the body where the hand joins the arm

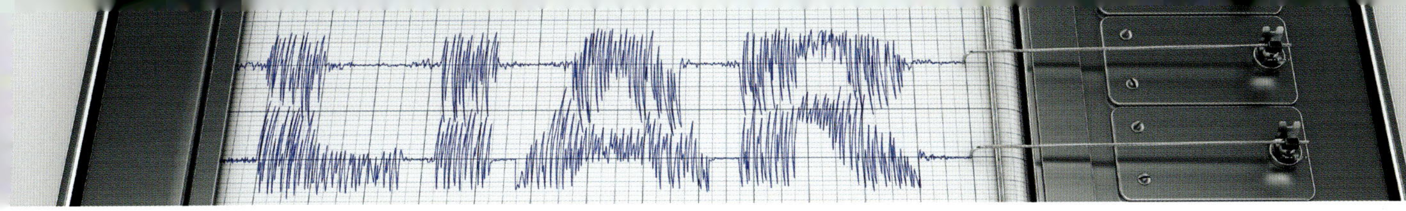

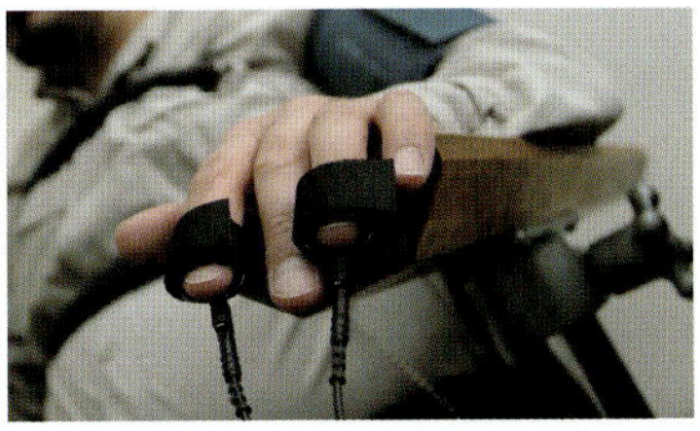

Polygraphs measure the moisture on your fingers.

As blood travels through the wrist, it creates very small sounds, and when subjects experience stress, the sounds become louder and faster. These sounds move the air in the tube, and the air pushes the bellows, moving the arm on the polygraph. A stronger, faster heart rate results in a more jagged line. Finally, the polygraph measures perspiration on the fingertips with metal plates called galvanometers, which are attached to two fingers. The galvanometers measure the skin's **conduction** of electricity. When people perspire, the skin becomes wet, and if subjects' skin is wetter than usual, it conducts more electricity. The galvanometers are connected to the third arm of the polygraph, and if the skin starts to increase in electrical conduction, movement of the arm increases. A comparison of the movements of all three arms should reveal to the examiner increases in stress for certain questions.

Many people debate the **reliability** of polygraphs. They believe that although these tests measure variations in the body associated with stress, these variations could be the result of other kinds of emotions. While some people experience **minimal** to no stress when lying, some honest people may experience intense stress from the exam itself. Because of this, it is possible for the examiner to wrongly deduce[8] that the subject is lying, and the subject might then be subjected[9] to unfair **punishment**. Even companies that produce polygraphs indicate that the mechanisms cannot detect lies, suggesting that polygraphs can only identify behavior that should not be trusted. Because of these criticisms, polygraph data cannot be used as evidence in American courts. Also, American law prohibits private companies from forcing employees to take polygraph tests. Despite this, both the American government and businesses continue to utilize polygraphs. In fact, workers for government agencies can be fired if they fail—or refuse to take—a polygraph test. Various opponents of polygraphs have concluded from this fact that the tests are used to intimidate workers, to make them confess to wrongdoing or prevent them from complaining about company policies. Regardless, it's clear that polygraph tests will continue to affect the lives of employees.

Q
What is this paragraph mainly about?
a. Reasons not to trust polygraph results
b. Ways to fool a polygraph

[8] **deduce** *v.* to conclude
[9] **subject** *v.* to force to undergo

READING COMPREHENSION

A Mark each statement as true (*T*) or false (*F*) according to the reading.

1 ______ A polygraph machine makes use of three styluses.

2 ______ Digital polygraph machines work completely differently from analog ones.

3 ______ The subject's heart rate is monitored using tubes around the wrists.

4 ______ Wet skin conducts more electricity than dry skin.

5 ______ Polygraph test results are admissible as evidence in US courts.

B Choose the best answer according to the reading.

1 What is the reading mainly about?

a. The difference between old and new polygraph machines
b. The problems with polygraph test accuracy
c. How polygraphs work and why they are controversial
d. How polygraphs were invented and why they were banned

2 Tubes around the subject's torso help to measure ______.

a. perspiration
b. heart rate
c. breathing rate
d. electricity

3 We can guess from paragraph 5 that ______.

a. some people can pass a polygraph test even if they are lying
b. polygraph tests very rarely result in false accusations
c. it is not normal to experience stress when lying
d. it is becoming easier to fake polygraph results

4 People can be required to take polygraph tests in American ______.

a. schools
b. courts
c. private companies
d. government agencies

SUMMARY

Fill in the blanks with the phrases in the box.

heart rate, etc.	falsely identify	detect deception
limited legally	reactions to stress	interview subjects

Institutions commonly use polygraphs to ❶ ________________, but they remain controversial.

Polygraphs are instruments that can detect physical ❷ ________________.

Critics point out the test may ❸ ________________ the reasons for stress.

Examiners ❹ ________________ with a series of carefully selected questions.

The polygraph machine measures changes in ❺ ________________.

Because of this, the use of test results has been ❻ ________________.

DISCUSSION

Discuss the following questions with your partner or classmates.

1 What would you do in the following situation? Why?

By cheating, some of your friends got A's on an important exam that you failed. In private, your teacher asks you if you know whether anyone cheated.

2 In what situations might it be better to lie than to tell the truth? Think of two or three situations and discuss them with a partner.

WRITING

Write a short paragraph answering the following question.

Q: Is it ever acceptable to lie?

☐ **[Opinion 1]** Yes, I think it is sometimes acceptable to lie.

☐ **[Opinion 2]** No, I do not think it is ever acceptable to lie.

Example

I think it is sometimes acceptable to lie. Being completely honest often means hurting others' feelings. It is simply cruel to tell someone that they look terrible or that their jokes aren't funny. And it does not accomplish anything. Furthermore, it is not wise to tell the truth if it puts someone else in danger. In such a situation, lying is morally necessary. It is true that when someone is caught in a lie, it can damage the liar's relationship with the person who was lied to. But many lies are minor and harmless, not serious betrayals of trust, and I consider these acceptable. While telling the truth is usually best, people need not feel guilty if they lie with no intention to hurt others or in order to protect another person.

My Paragraph

Reading 2 Return of the Con Artist: Tips to Protect Yourself

BEFORE YOU READ

Talk about these questions with your classmates.

What skills do you think criminals have that make their scams effective? Think of at least two and discuss them with a partner.

Think About It

How can people avoid being victims of scams?

VOCABULARY PREVIEW

Choose the one that is closest to the meaning of the word in bold.

1 The **unprincipled** people who commit these crimes are hard to detect.
a. incapable b. uneducated c. immoral

2 **Manipulative** criminals are good at convincing their victims to do what they want.
a. showing nervousness b. able to control people c. knowledgeable

3 Criminals take advantage of people's fears and **insecurities**.
a. anger about unfairness b. doubts about oneself c. personal secrets

4 What can people do to protect themselves from **exploitation**?
a. being falsely accused b. being distrusted c. being used unfairly

5 Instead of being emotional, try to maintain your **objectivity**.
a. rationality b. generosity c. personality

Return of the Con Artist: Tips to Protect Yourself

by Dr. George Simon, Ph.D.

Q Why have some types of fraud increased lately?

In a poor economy, it can get pretty hard to make an honest living. That's possibly why con artists appear to be making a sort of comeback these days. Of course, they have always been around; but when times get tough, reports of people being victimized by these dishonest characters increase.

Recently, a large Christian congregation[1] in Canada was the target of a scam[2] in which they lost their school and day care center. And in another province, a con artist got over thirty people to pay $1,000 each toward an apartment he didn't even own. By some reports, con games are on the rise in the business world as well. In total, mortgage and land frauds[3], identity thefts, and various other tricks have cost developed economies billions over the past decade. There are some indications that, overall, small frauds of various types are actually on the decline, but the number of larger (and lucrative[4]) "superfrauds" has definitely increased in recent years. And while the very nature of the typical schemes and the **unprincipled** "artists" who conduct them makes them hard to detect, there are some things you can watch out for.

What is a con artist, exactly? The term *con* is short for "confidence." These **manipulative** thieves are particularly skilled in getting you to ignore any hesitancy[5] you might have, and thereby secure your confidence. As soon as they've gotten your trust, you're ready to take the inevitable fall that lies ahead. Sometimes, "running the con" takes only a few short minutes, and you only know what's happened long after the damage has already been done and the con artist is gone. Other cons take a longer time to carry out successfully. Generally speaking, the more money involved in the plan, the longer it takes to set up.

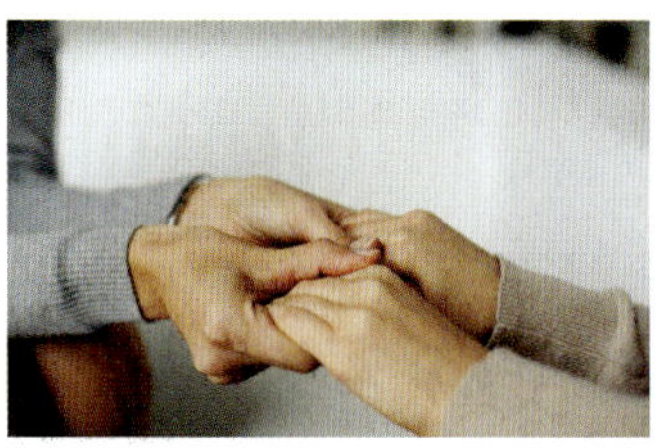

Dishonest people may use your compassion against you.

Q Underline three types of people's vulnerabilities that con artists make use of.

How do these criminals gain your trust in the first place? By preying on your greatest vulnerabilities[6]. Sometimes, those vulnerabilities are your good qualities, like your trusting nature or your compassionate[7] heart. Other times, it's your fears and **insecurities** that they take advantage of. But they can also use your character flaws, such as greed, envy, and vanity. Skilled con artists start evaluating your character from the very first moment they see you, taking note of your personality, your likes and dislikes, and especially any weakness in your ability to correctly judge the character of others.

1 **congregation** *n.* a religious community
2 **scam** *n.* a way to make money by deceiving people; *v.* to deceive in order to take others' money
3 **fraud** *n.* a deception; a trick
4 **lucrative** *adj.* profitable
5 **hesitancy** *n.* reluctance; doubt
6 **vulnerability** *n.* a weakness (vulnerable *adj.*)
7 **compassionate** *adj.* kind; concerned about others' suffering

Is there anything you can do to protect yourself from this kind of **exploitation**? Some con artists are so skilled and charming that it's almost impossible to avoid being fooled by them. But there are some things you can do to improve the chances that you won't be a victim. First of all, you need to accept the fact that we live in an era when a lack of integrity is fairly common, so you always need to be on your guard. Never take anyone or anything at face value. And do your homework. Check things out. Verify[8]. Information is power. The more you know, the less likely you'll be taken for a ride[9]. Additionally, look for the following warning signs:

1. Beware of shallowness and smooth-talking charm. Con artists are great at using words and at making wonderful first impressions. But their charm is generally only on the surface. Their history of relationships is likely to be troubled, and it's often hard to find anyone who can assure you of their honesty. The more you find out about them, the less appealing they're likely to appear. Maintain your **objectivity**, and look for clear evidence that your interests are being respected. Talk, as they say, is cheap.

Con artists tend to be charming and make great first impressions.

2. Pay attention to any uncomfortable feelings you might have or the little voice in your head that says something just doesn't add up or sound quite right. Don't be afraid to ask questions, especially follow-up questions, even if the other person tries to make you feel overly suspicious for doing so. Many con artists lie so liberally and with such ease that they'll sometimes make a mistake and expose their cons accidentally. Listen very carefully, and maybe you'll get an idea of what the real agenda[10] might be.

Q Circle three pieces of advice in this paragraph.

3. Know yourself. Be aware of the kinds of things that would make you susceptible[11] to becoming a victim. Acknowledge your fears and insecurities, your deepest desires, and especially your vices[12]. Keep in mind the old saying: if something sounds too good to be true, it probably is. Often, the things that sound the sweetest to our ears are the things that either relieve our fears or appeal to our worst instincts.

Just recently, a man with a troubled past and a heroin addiction scammed another man out of $133,000 over the period of a year by claiming he needed the money to cover medical expenses for a severely ill child. The con man knew that his story wasn't really very convincing and was surprised by how easy the con was to run. But his target was a Catholic priest with a big and trusting heart, who was just too vulnerable. And although $133,000 is a lot (including all of the priest's personal savings and a large portion of his church's funds), it's hard to say what the greater crime is: the loss of all that money or a kind man's loss of faith in the basic goodness of humankind.

C What is the author's main purpose in this passage?
(1) To entertain
(2) To inform
(3) To persuade

---

8 **verify** *v.* to make sure something is true
9 **be taken for a ride** *idiom* to be fooled
10 **agenda** *n.* an underlying plan or goal
11 **susceptible** *adj.* easily influenced or affected
12 **vice** *n.* a bad habit; a character flaw

READING COMPREHENSION

A Organize the ideas from the reading. Review the passage and fill in the graphic organizer below.

Return of the con artist

- "Superfrauds" have [1] ________________ lately.
- "Con" is short for "[2] ________________": criminals will try to gain your trust.

- Con artists use your good qualities, bad qualities, and your [3] ________________.

To protect yourself:

- Always be on your guard and check facts.
- Be suspicious of people who are [4] ________________.
- Listen and ask questions.
- Be aware of your own [5] ________________.

Scams cost people both their money and their faith in humankind.

B Choose the best answer according to the reading.

1 What can be inferred about con artists from paragraph 4?

a. They can guess how much money people make just by looking at them.
b. They are skilled at identifying people's weaknesses.
c. They usually become friends with people before trying to con them.
d. They tend to target very self-confident people.

2 What is the main idea of paragraph 6?

a. Despite their charm, you can often identify con artists by researching them.
b. Con artists are generally lonely people with few friends.
c. Con artists are skillful liars, and they are good at making people like them.
d. You should not give people personal information until you are sure of their honesty.

SUMMARY

Fill in the blanks with the phrases in the box.

ask questions	trusting nature	lucrative "superfrauds"
seems charming	dishonest characters	be aware

The number of small frauds may be declining, but ❶ ________________ such as mortgage and land frauds have recently increased. The "con" in "con artist" is short for "confidence," because these ❷ ________________ trick people into giving them their confidence and trust. They do this by taking advantage of a person's ❸ ________________, fears, insecurities, or character flaws such as greed. To protect yourself, always stay on your guard and ❹ ________________. Do not trust someone simply because he or she ❺ ________________. Listen carefully and ask questions. Also, ❻ ________________ of your own weaknesses and vices. Remember that if something sounds too good to be true, it probably is.

DISCUSSION

A **Read this excerpt from the reading passage.**

Return of the Con Artist: Tips to Protect Yourself

How do these criminals gain your trust in the first place? By preying on your greatest vulnerabilities. Sometimes, those vulnerabilities are your good qualities, like your trusting nature or your compassionate heart. Other times, it's your fears and insecurities that they take advantage of. But they can also use your character flaws, such as greed, envy, and vanity.

B **Discuss the following questions with your partner or classmates.**

1. Which of the above types of scams do you think is the most effective? Why?
2. Describe scams that make use of (a) people's compassion, (b) people's fears, and (c) people's greed.

WRITING

Write a short paragraph answering the following question.

Q: What can people do to avoid being victims of con artists?

☐ **[Opinion]** To avoid being victims of con artists, people should guard their weaknesses, ____________________, and ____________________.

Example

To avoid being victims of con artists, people should guard their weaknesses, ask plenty of questions, and do research on their destinations if they are traveling. People must constantly beware of con artists' tendency to prey on their targets' weaknesses. If an offer involving money seems too good to be true, it is probably a scam that is meant to take advantage of people's greed. People should find out as much as possible about any person or organization before giving them money. If it is an individual, ask for references. If it is a charity, find out how exactly the donation will be used. Before making a trip abroad, people should research what scams are directed at tourists where they are going. Tourists who are unfamiliar with the local area are popular targets for con artists, but knowledge is power. Con artists are clever, but people can avoid becoming victims by being cautious, being aware of con artists' tricks, and being thorough in their research.

My Paragraph

Unit 6 • Psychology

Reading 1 Horror Movies Haunt Us Long after They're Over

BEFORE YOU READ

Talk about these questions with your classmates.

1 Why do you think some people enjoy watching scary movies while others are bothered by them?
2 Can you remember a movie that scared you as a child? Do you think it would still scare you if you watched it today?

Think About It

What is your opinion of horror movies? Are they harmless fun, or not so harmless?

VOCABULARY PREVIEW

Match each word in bold with its meaning in the box.

a. be one cause of	b. watch	c. separate
d. however	e. nervousness	

_____ **1** Frightening movies usually create a sense of **tension** among viewers.

_____ **2** Some forgot the scary movie soon afterward, **whereas** others remembered it for years.

_____ **3** Brain scans allowed scientists to **isolate** the areas of the brain that were most active.

_____ **4** Watching too much TV as a young child can **contribute** to problems later in life.

_____ **5** The researchers **monitored** the children while they viewed a few different scenes.

Horror Movies Haunt Us Long after They're Over

by Meredith Richards

When I was 7, I went to a slumber party[1] where we watched a couple of horror movies. In one of them, a man who was murdered at sea returns as a zombie to get revenge on his killers. I was old enough to know that movies weren't real. I was even familiar with the star actor, a likable guy known mostly for comedy roles. Yet he scared me out of my wits[2]. For weeks afterward as I tried to go to sleep, some small part of my 7-year-old brain believed he would show up in my room as the walking dead, dripping water and seaweed. Needless to say, there were some sleepless nights. And that frightening image is just as vivid[3] to me now, decades later.

Q Which two sentences state the main idea of the passage? Underline them.

Fans of the genre[4] like to say that horror movies are all in good fun—harmless entertainment. They might even tease kids who are frightened by these movies for being "wimps[5]" or "wusses[6]." But as my experience suggests, there are unwanted psychological effects linked to watching horror movies, particularly for children. And these effects can last far beyond a few weeks of sleeping with the lights on.

Q Find five effects of scary movies on young kids that the author mentions. Circle them.

Not everything on TV is suitable for the whole family.

Even kids who are too young to understand the content of a scary movie can be significantly upset by it. Children under the age of about 5 cannot tell fantasy from reality. This makes violent on-screen images both confusing and disturbing for them. A 2006 study found that, for toddlers, even the scary music and the sense of **tension** among the other viewers in the room can be sufficient to cause anxiety, nightmares, and aggressive behavior in the period right after viewing a horror film. In fact, too much TV and movie viewing is unhealthy for toddlers in general. It interferes with brain development and can **contribute** to ADHD. Experts in pediatric[7] psychology, such as Dr. Daniel Schechter of Columbia University, recommend no more than thirty minutes a day for children under 6.

Horror movies have a negative impact on older children as well, and the effects can last into adulthood. In 1999, some researchers surveyed 150 college students about their

1 **slumber party** *n.* a party at which partygoers sleep overnight at the host's home
2 **out of one's wits** *idiom* not in control of one's thoughts and emotions because of great fear
3 **vivid** *adj.* very clear
4 **genre** *n.* a type (of movie, book, etc.)
5 **wimp** *n.* a weak person who lacks courage
6 **wuss** *n.* a coward; someone easily scared
7 **pediatric** *adj.* relating to children

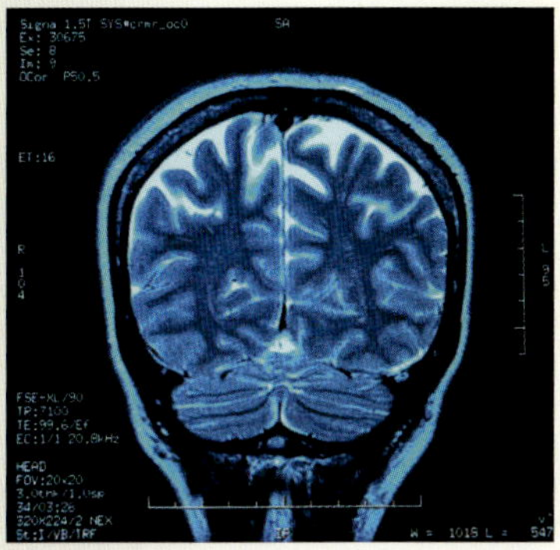

MRIs are helping us understand what scary movies do to our brains.

experiences with horror movies. Ninety percent reported having been frightened by a horror film when they were children or teens. The average age of the experience was 14. Symptoms included nightmares (of course), crying, shaking, nausea, and fear of dying. Most reported having trouble sleeping or other behavior disruptions[8] as a result of watching the scary movie. But perhaps most concerning was how long the effects lasted for a significant number of the students. **Whereas** some said they were fine after a week, twenty-six percent said they still felt "residual[9] anxiety" from the scary images. And half of the students reported a continuing fear and avoidance of something associated with the film, such as the sight of blood—whether in real life or on the screen. Phobias[10] produced in this way can last a lifetime, according to researchers. (You have to wonder how many potentially brilliant doctors the world has lost to horror movies.)

C Underline the results of the study discussed in this paragraph. Do they support the author's main point in this paragraph?

Why do frightening scenes affect us so powerfully? The problem is that even when we know a scary image is not real, our brains and bodies react as if it were. That physical reaction is the same reason some people find violent movies such fun to watch. Our heart and breathing rates increase; our palms sweat and our muscles tense; we gasp and cover our eyes. Brain scans show how this works. A research team used functional MRI to **monitor** the brains of fifteen children between the ages of 8 and 12 as they watched three different videos: a scene from a children's show, a nature scene, and a violent scene. Thus, the researchers were able to **isolate** the different parts of the kids' brains that were active during the different videos. Compared with the non-violent scenes, the violent one produced more activity in the center for emotional processing and in the amygdala, where the fear reflex[11] is located. Significantly, the center for memory storage was also more active, indicating that we find violent images more memorable. This result helps explain why scary movies can have such lasting emotional consequences.

So no matter how old you are, don't be embarrassed about saying no when your friends suggest a horror movie marathon. You may be ensuring sweeter dreams for everyone that night. You could even be protecting your psyche[12] as well as theirs from the triggering of terrifying childhood memories. And, please, if you ever host a slumber party for 7-year-olds, stick to *Finding Nemo*.

C Which best describes the author's purpose in this paragraph?
(1) To entertain
(2) To persuade
(3) To inform

8 **disruption** *n.* a problem; a difficulty
9 **residual** *adj.* leftover; remaining
10 **phobia** *n.* an irrational fear
11 **reflex** *n.* an unthinking physical reaction
12 **psyche** *n.* one's mind and deepest feelings and attitudes

READING COMPREHENSION

Choose the best answer according to the reading.

1 What is the main point the author makes about horror movies in the passage?

a. It is OK to refuse to watch them.
b. They are inappropriate for children under 14.
c. People respond to them as if they were really in danger.
d. They have a long-term negative impact on many people's minds.

2 What kind of support does the author mainly give for the main idea of the article?

a. Scientific studies
b. Interviews with experts
c. Explanations and definitions
d. Personal experience

3 What can we infer about toddlers from the passage?

a. They should not watch an entire movie at one time.
b. They can benefit from watching a lot of educational shows.
c. They are fine around horror movies as long as they don't see the screen.
d. They are not upset by scary movies if their parents are nearby.

4 Which of the following is NOT true about the students surveyed in the 1999 study?

a. Most had found a movie frightening earlier in their lives.
b. Some of them had no long-lasting effects from the scary film.
c. The majority reported problems like sleeplessness and crying.
d. Very few of them still avoided something associated with the movie.

5 How did the researchers study the reactions of the fifteen children to violent images?

a. By measuring the kids' heart rates while they watched a violent scene
b. By taking images of the kids' brains while they watched different videos
c. By asking the kids which scenes they remembered best
d. By asking the kids how different videos affected them

SUMMARY

Write the number of each sentence under the category it belongs to.

Watching Horror Movies	
Negative Impacts	Reasons for those Impacts

1. Horror movies make children under the age of 5 feel confused and disturbed because they cannot tell fantasy from reality.
2. The scary music in horror movies can cause anxiety, nightmares, and even aggressive behavior.
3. Ninety percent of 150 college students had trouble sleeping or other behavior disruptions as a result of watching scary movies.
4. Although adults know a scary image is not real, their brains and bodies react as if it were.
5. According to research, some people experienced a continuing fear and avoidance of something associated with horror movies, such as the sight of blood.

DISCUSSION

Discuss the following questions with your partner or classmates.

1 What kinds of rules should parents make concerning their kids and horror movies?

2 How does the government restrict young people from watching horror movies? Are these restrictions effective?

WRITING

Write a short paragraph answering the following question.

Q: Do you think horror movies are harmful and should be avoided?

☐ **[Opinion 1]** Yes, I think horror movies are harmful and should be avoided.

☐ **[Opinion 2]** No, I think horror movies are harmless fun that people should enjoy.

Example

Yes, I think horror movies are harmful and should be avoided. These films seriously upset young children. Even being in the same room as people watching a horror movie can make toddlers anxious and aggressive. Horror movies can also have long-term emotional effects. A study found that many college students still felt anxiety that was linked to a movie they had seen years before. Some people claim to enjoy horror films and not suffer any negative consequences. However, I think that watching horrible violence makes these people less sensitive to it in real life, which is a problem. Because of the obvious harm they can cause to people's emotional health, I think everyone would be better off staying away from horror movies.

My Paragraph

Unit 6 • Psychology

Reading 2 Hooray for Pessimism

BEFORE YOU READ

Talk about these questions with your classmates.

1 How might being an optimist affect your health positively? Negatively? What about being a pessimist?
2 In what kinds of situations can expecting the worst be helpful? Think of at least one example and discuss it with a partner.

Think About It

Are there advantages to being optimistic or pessimistic?

VOCABULARY PREVIEW

Choose the one that is closest to the meaning of the word in bold.

a. a reason for doing something
b. relating to the use of machines
c. to move forward; to continue
d. a future chance; an opportunity for the future
e. the chances of something happening; probability

_____ **1** I am not usually hopeful about my **prospects** of a bright future.

_____ **2** Against the **odds**, sometimes good things do happen.

_____ **3** Stress about the future can be a **motivation** to act.

_____ **4** You might expect **technical** problems with your computer.

_____ **5** People who think everything will **proceed** smoothly might not prepare for problems.

Hooray for Pessimism

by Regina Lalonde

"Think positive!" "Look on the bright side!" "Smile! Everything will work out in the end!" These words of advice—commands, really—come my way on a regular basis, from family, friends, co-workers, and even total strangers. You see, I'm a pessimist. I wouldn't describe myself as unhappy; however, at any given moment, I'm more likely to be frowning in thought about what might go wrong next than I am to be smiling at the **prospect** of a bright future. This puts me in the minority in a culture that practically worships positive thinking. Hence, the constant orders from those around me to be more optimistic. Since pessimism is in my nature, I couldn't obey them if I wanted to. But I don't want to. Despite the social and health benefits of optimism, which are no doubt real to some degree, I've learned that pessimism is greatly underrated[1]. A healthy amount of such negativity can actually benefit a person emotionally, professionally, and financially.

Q Why does the author describe herself as "in the minority"?

Pessimism takes many forms, but the relevant ones here are dispositional and defensive pessimism. (Think "disposition" as in "personality.") In psychology, dispositional pessimism is the personality trait of having generally low expectations. In other words, a dispositional pessimist may not know what's going to happen, but he or she is pretty sure it won't be anything great.

C Circle the term that is defined in this paragraph. Underline the definition.

Although this sounds like a dreary[2] way to go through life, dispositional pessimism might lead to stronger, longer-lasting relationships. Several recent studies have found that negativity has a positive effect on couples because it prepares them for the worst. One study followed eighty-two married couples and found that when they encountered difficulties it was the optimists that suffered most because their disappointment was "extreme and often irrational." By trying to be relentlessly[3] positive, they actually harmed their relationships. In contrast, the dispositional pessimists accepted some trouble as normal, and thus were able to deal with it. According to the lead researcher, these couples ended up with more successful and satisfying marriages as a result.

Couples with lower expectations seem to deal with conflict better.

A bit of dispositional pessimism comes in handy at work as well. Dr. Aaron Sackett, Ph.D., is a psychologist at the University of St. Thomas in St. Paul and a critic of what he calls the "cult[4]" of optimism. As he explained to *Psychology Today*, if an optimist is denied an expected promotion, he or she will feel both shocked and crushed. A pessimist in the same situation never had his or her hopes up[5] to begin with, and therefore will not be nearly so deeply affected. Pessimists, then, have built-in ego protection. Since disappointment is

Q The author uses a hypothetical situation to illustrate the point of this paragraph. Underline it.

---

1 **underrated** *adj.* not valued enough
2 **dreary** *adj.* depressing
3 **relentlessly** *adv.* without stopping or giving up
4 **cult** *n.* a false and often dangerous religion
5 **get / have one's hopes up** *idiom* to become hopeful

inevitable in any career, the pessimist's way does appear wiser. As a bonus, pessimists are especially delighted when, against all **odds**, good things do happen. "Optimists never get the joy of a pleasant surprise," Sackett points out.

Defensive pessimism benefits people in more concrete[6] ways. It is useful to view it as dispositional pessimism applied to specific situations: It is the tendency to be anxious about what could go wrong and to use that anxiety as **motivation** to act.

The advantages of this in the workplace are pretty obvious. Say you are a pessimist in charge of organizing an important presentation. You'll expect **technical** problems, so you'll set up and test the computer equipment in advance. You'll fear that additional people might show up, so you'll have extra copies of the handouts ready. And you'll worry that the meeting will run longer than expected, so you'll arrange for snacks to be delivered. Through the power of negative thinking, you will be much better prepared than the optimist who assumes everything will **proceed** smoothly. Now, granted, research suggests that optimists are more likely to be hired and are quicker to be promoted. To me, this merely confirms what I already knew—that people usually prefer being around optimists because of their sunny personalities. Significantly, what this research does not prove is that a positive outlook actually makes someone a better or more efficient worker. The opposite seems more likely to be true.

C The author raises a possible objection to the argument in this paragraph. Underline it.

Optimistic gamblers are sure they'll win—even when they're losing.

Defensive pessimism seems to lead to more prudent[7] money management, too. One interesting experiment involved observing college students as they gambled at simulated card games and slot machines. Those who had scored high on a test of optimism were more likely to believe they would win—and they believed this even more strongly after they had lost money—leading to further losses. Only the pessimistic students reduced their bets after losing, which is surely the logical thing to do. A similar principle could be observed on a global scale following the 2008 world financial crisis, which made defensive pessimists out of millions of people. Since then, people in many affected countries have felt increased anxiety about their financial futures and have adjusted their behavior accordingly, saving more for retirement and avoiding disastrous credit card debt.

C Is the argument in this paragraph inductive or deductive?

Considering how pessimism can prevent disappointment, shield[8] one's ego, and protect against job-related or financial misfortunes, one would think it would be more widely accepted. Dr. Julie Norem, Ph.D., who specializes in this area, told the *Huffington Post*: "There's an awful lot of pressure for people to present themselves as optimistic, and it probably causes more pain than the pessimism itself." Norem adds that the dominance of optimism may be coming to an end, and soon there may be a "broad cultural shift" toward more negativity. Maybe, but I'm not getting my hopes up.

---

6 **concrete** *adj.* involving specific people, situations, etc., and not ideas or qualities

7 **prudent** *adj.* careful and sensible

8 **shield** *v.* to protect

READING COMPREHENSION

Choose the best answer according to the reading.

1 What is the main idea of paragraph 3?

a. Married couples usually become more pessimistic over time.
b. Pessimism helps relationships by keeping expectations realistic.
c. Pessimists are more cautious about whom they marry.
d. Most newly married couples are optimistic about the future.

2 According to paragraph 4, pessimists are ______________.

a. less likely to have big egos
b. less likely to ask for promotions
c. more likely to be promoted
d. more happily surprised when things go well

3 What can be inferred about defensive pessimism?

a. It is useful in stressful situations.
b. It is generally only displayed at work.
c. It may be a disadvantage in one's social life.
d. It is less common than dispositional pessimism.

4 According to paragraph 6, studies show that optimists ______________.

a. stay at the same job longer
b. are preferred by employers
c. take more risks in their careers
d. have poorer job performance on average

5 According to paragraph 7, what has the 2008 financial crisis demonstrated?

a. The impossibility of predicting economic trends
b. The difficulty of changing one's money habits
c. The benefits of defensive pessimism
d. The carelessness of most optimists

SUMMARY

An introductory sentence for a brief summary of the passage is provided below. Select THREE more sentences to complete the summary.

First Sentence: A certain amount of pessimism can have benefits in various areas of life.

1. Pessimists accept that problems are normal and they therefore have stronger relationships.
2. According to research, optimists have an advantage in hiring and promotion.
3. Pessimists are less affected by disappointments at work and more prepared to deal with things that go wrong.
4. Optimists take risks with money, while pessimism often leads to sensible financial decisions.
5. "Dispositional pessimism" refers to pessimism as a personality trait, while "defensive pessimism" applies to specific situations.
6. There is a good deal of social pressure for people to present themselves as optimistic.

DISCUSSION

Discuss the following questions with your partner or classmates.

1 In what ways do you think being a pessimist can be harmful to a career?

2 Think of the last time you had to do something stressful. Did you practice "defensive pessimism"? Explain.

WRITING

Write a short paragraph answering the following question.

Q: In your opinion, is it better to be an optimist or a pessimist?

☐ **[Opinion 1]** I think it is better to be an optimist.

☐ **[Opinion 2]** I think it is a better idea to be a pessimist.

Example

I think it is a better idea to be a pessimist. Pessimists probably live longer. Because they tend to expect the worst, pessimists are more likely to see a doctor if they think something is wrong. This can save their lives. Pessimists are better prepared when things go wrong. Defensive pessimism makes people plan for problems and bad luck, and this planning can prevent disaster. Pessimists are more careful with their money. Unlike optimists, who are more likely to take risks with their money because they believe things will turn out well, pessimists are less likely to lose money by gambling or by making unwise financial decisions. Evidence shows that optimists tend to have more friends because of their sunny personality. However, it is possible to be a pessimist when it comes to planning for the future and still be a happy, sociable person. In many ways, pessimism prepares a person for life's challenges better than optimism does.

My Paragraph

Unit 7 • Lifestyles

Reading 1 How I Learned to Stop Apologizing for Being Vegetarian

BEFORE YOU READ

Talk about these questions with your classmates.

How common are vegetarians in your country? What difficulties do they face, if any? Discuss with a partner.

VOCABULARY PREVIEW

Choose the one that is closest to the meaning of the word in bold.

1 Our gardener thought it was wrong to hurt animals just because you could, and his **logic** made sense to me.
a. feeling b. reasoning c. evidence

2 My daughter and I worked together to **draft** a letter to the school.
a. write b. answer c. revise

3 It was **inevitable** that she would ask more questions as she got older.
a. unforgivable b. unpredictable c. unavoidable

4 After starting a farm, the practice of killing a goat is to celebrate its **subsequent** success.
a. past b. major c. later

5 I was afraid to enter Kibera during the violence; **nevertheless**, I wanted to help.
a. in other words b. still c. also

How I Learned to Stop Apologizing for Being Vegetarian 13

by JC Niala

It is an argument used by parents of picky eaters the world over: "Think of the starving[1] children in Africa." But in Kenya, where those starving children can be found on your doorstep, this argument applies to nearly anyone who chooses to limit the food he or she eats. When I tell people that I am a vegetarian[2], they assume it must be for medical reasons. Why else would an African woman who can afford to eat meat refuse what so many of her fellow citizens don't have the luxury[3] of turning down?

My reasoning, however, stretches back to when I was a little girl, growing up on my parents' estate, surrounded by animals both domestic and wild. Having gotten to know them as I did, it was not hard to imagine how greatly they suffered when taken to the slaughterhouse[4]. Such thoughts made me view the meat that I ate differently. Yet when I tried to talk with adults about it, I was told that animals were different, or that God provided them for us to eat. The only person who told me otherwise was our gardener, who was against hurting any animal (even a deadly Black Mamba snake) just because you could.

Growing up on a farm in Kenya, her home country, the author was told animals existed for humans to eat.

Q What two reasons did adults give the author for eating meat? Circle them.

While his **logic** persuaded[5] me, it would take another decade for me to truly become a vegetarian. And even then, I hardly dared admit it was because of my larger commitment to nonviolence. Recently, however, thanks to my 5-year-old daughter, I've begun to examine my own inaction when it comes to animal rights.

In January 2008, when Kenya was rocked by post-election violence, Kibera—the neighborhood just across the road from where I live in Nairobi—was hit the hardest. I had always been scared to enter Kibera, Africa's largest poor urban area. **Nevertheless**, I decided to venture[6] among the burning tires to see what I could do to help.

Although it seems naive[7] to me now, I felt that a large part of people's frustrations were based on not being able to feed their families. So with the help of an inspiring youth

1 **starving** *adj.* lacking enough food to live
2 **vegetarian** *n.* one who does not eat meat; *adj.* relating to a vegetarian
3 **luxury** *n.* something welcome but not usually available or affordable
4 **slaughterhouse** *n.* a building in which animals are killed for meat
5 **persuade** *v.* to convince
6 **venture** *v.* to dare to go
7 **naive** *adj.* showing a lack of knowledge and experience; simple

group, I started an organic[8] vegetable farm in the heart of Kibera. Although normally there would have been a symbolic killing of a goat to celebrate the farm's **subsequent** success, my newly acquired friends understood that I would not pay for an animal to be killed. Still, they laughed at what to them seemed like a very odd diet because I never fully explained to them why I had completely stopped eating meat.

Q Why did the author start a vegetable farm? Underline her reason.

Over the next few years, my inhibitions[9] about raising a vegetarian child in a meat-eating culture kept me from talking about my choice. Although my daughter knew we were vegetarian, I never really told her why, and she never really asked. It all came to a head[10] when a family friend offered her a rib at a barbecue. Without any hesitation, she refused and said loudly that she didn't eat animals because they were her friends. People thought it was cute.

The author's daughter thinks of animals as her friends.

I soon started to write down her answers to the **inevitable** questions, which increased as she grew older. Unlike her mother, she did not apologize for being a vegetarian. She talked about why she didn't think it was right to hurt animals. Eventually, these quotes formed the basis[11] of a book about being vegetarian that we published recently, called *Cows Are Too Big to Eat*.

C What is the author's point of view on her daughter's behavior?
(1) Amused
(2) Admiring
(3) Angry

It did not end there. When the board at her small community-run school announced that they were going to introduce meat into the previously vegetarian menu, my daughter spoke up again. I was taken by surprise, but I wasn't willing to cause too much trouble. However, when I discussed it with my daughter, she said, "Mama, what are we going to do about it?"

Noting that her response had included "we," I asked for her comments so that I could **draft** a letter to the board. She asked me to write that if they were worried about protein, then the children could eat cheese and drink milk. Thus, a cow would not have to be killed. The board responded by doing a survey, which led to a reversal[12] of the decision to introduce meat into the school, at least for the kindergarteners.

Q What two things happened as a result of the letter to the board? Underline them.

It's hard to say if my daughter will take up the fight again next year when she moves on to primary school. Like most children, she lives firmly in the present. But that's OK. It's me who is thinking about the future. And going forward, I know that I will no longer be ashamed to say why I am vegetarian. It took nearly two decades, but thanks to my daughter I make no apologies for wanting to live a life of nonviolence, with respect toward all animals.

8 **organic** *adj.* grown or raised naturally
9 **inhibition** *n.* a feeling of shyness or unwillingness
10 **come to a head** *idiom* to reach a critical point
11 **basis** *n.* origin; something from which something else develops
12 **reversal** *n.* the act of changing to the opposite direction, decision, etc.

READING COMPREHENSION

A **Organize the ideas from the reading. Review the passage and fill in the graphic organizer below.**

Learning to stop apologizing for being vegetarian

As a child, the author got to know animals and could imagine how they [1] ________ ________.

The author helped to start [2] ________ in 2008.

The author and her daughter worked together on [3] ________ about vegetarianism.

The author and her daughter wrote a letter opposing [4] ________ ________.

Finally, the author decided to stop [5] ________ ________.

B **Choose the best answer according to the reading.**

1 When the author was a child, the gardener ________.

a. told her that animals live for humans to eat
b. made her feel ashamed for caring about animals
c. agreed with her that animals should not suffer
d. explained that animals are not like humans

2 What can be inferred about the members of the youth group the author worked with in Kibera?

a. They were not vegetarians.
b. They were fairly wealthy.
c. They were victims of violence.
d. They were not originally from Kibera.

SUMMARY

Fill in the blanks with the phrases in the box.

to speak up	no longer	with her daughter
surrounded by animals	belief in nonviolence	school menu

The writer, a Kenyan woman, had thought about the suffering of animals since she was a child ❶ __________. Later she became a vegetarian due to her ❷ __________. She raised her daughter as a vegetarian but did not fully explain why, because she lived in a meat-eating culture. Then her young daughter began ❸ __________ about her own concern for animals. ❹ __________, the writer authored a book called *Cows Are Too Big to Eat*. The mother and daughter also became involved in activism, working to keep the local ❺ __________ vegetarian. Because of her daughter, the writer ❻ __________ apologizes for her beliefs.

DISCUSSION

A **Read the excerpt from the reading passage.**

How I Learned to Stop Apologizing for Being Vegetarian

Although my daughter knew we were vegetarian, I never really told her why, and she never really asked. It all came to a head when a family friend offered her a rib at a barbecue. Without any hesitation, she refused and said loudly that she didn't eat animals because they were her friends. People thought it was cute.

B **Discuss the following questions with your partner or classmates.**

1 Do you think the little girl's reason for being vegetarian is a good one?

2 What are some other reasons people become vegetarians? Which reason do you consider the best?

WRITING

Write a short paragraph answering the following question.

Q: Do you think it is morally acceptable to eat meat?

☐ **[Opinion 1]** Yes, I think it is morally acceptable to eat meat.

☐ **[Opinion 2]** No, I do not think it is morally acceptable to eat meat.

Example

I do not think it is morally acceptable to eat meat. Animals killed for meat experience pain and suffering. Factory farms keep animals indoors in small cages for their entire lives. Eating meat is also bad for the environment. Animal farming produces a lot of pollution and uses up too many resources. Furthermore, meat is not necessary for a healthy diet. By choosing foods carefully and taking vitamin supplements, vegetarians can be perfectly healthy. Advocates of eating meat claim that it is OK because many animals besides humans do it. Unlike other animals, humans can think about right and wrong and make moral choices. There is no moral justification for using animals as food, and everyone should switch to a vegetarian diet.

My Paragraph

Unit 7 • Lifestyles

Reading 2 Generation Boomerang: Children Who Go Back to Mom and Dad

BEFORE YOU READ

Talk about these questions with your classmates.

This passage is an online magazine article about young adults in the UK who are moving back in with their parents. What problems do you think could occur when adults live with their parents? Think of at least two and discuss them with a partner.

Think About It

Is it a good idea for people in their twenties and thirties to live with their parents?

VOCABULARY PREVIEW

Choose the one that is closest to the meaning of the word in bold.

1 Today's students will finish college with **unprecedented** levels of debt.
   a. hard to imagine b. never seen before c. impossible to pay

2 Lending **institutions** are more cautious about offering mortgages.
   a. organizations b. financial regulations c. experts

3 It's comforting for young people to move in with their **devoted** parents.
   a. familiar b. happy c. loving

4 Living with parents might prevent a person from reaching true **maturity**.
   a. adulthood b. satisfaction c. success

5 People cannot be **reliant** on their moms and dads forever.
   a. critical b. similar c. dependent

Generation Boomerang:
Children Who Go Back to Mom and Dad

14

by Sally Koslow and Hannah Booth

When my husband and I learned that, at 25, one son would be returning to live with us again, we initially expected his stay to last perhaps two months. Then he lost his job. Months passed, and we found ourselves unable to stay silent. "Have you updated your résumé? While you're at it, could you please do your laundry, clean up, and walk the dog?" Eventually, with a shove[1], our son reluctantly accepted a job and moved out.

A decade later, the number of "adultescents" living in their parents' homes has increased apace[2], victims of a slow economy. According to the Office for National Statistics, nearly three million British adults aged 20 to 34 lived with their parents in 2011, up twenty percent since 1997. More than one million under-25s are now unemployed; and with the introduction of higher tuition fees, future students should expect to finish their degree with **unprecedented** debts of up to £60,000. Lending **institutions** are shying away from offering mortgages[3], and house prices have risen beyond the realms[4] of possibility for many young people.

Q Underline all the reasons given in the paragraph why young British people are struggling financially.

Boomerang kids might view living at home as a long vacation.

These experiences may result in a severe hit to self-esteem; returning home to **devoted** parents can sometimes soothe[5] that wound. Many young adults, however, exist in a cloud of overconfidence, with an illusion of endless time. "This is a more entitled generation than their parents' and grandparents'," says William J. Doherty, professor of family social science. "We're seeing young adults tethered[6] to family in the sense that they live at home, but with no major responsibility to work as contributing members."

Q What adjective is used to describe the young generation in this paragraph? Circle it.

Today's parents tend to treat young adults like pampered[7] teens, reinvesting in dormant[8] parenting roles, especially if their kids are struggling. "The underlying message is 'We don't think you can do it on your own,'" says Marie Hartwell-Walker, psychologist and mother of four adult children, two of whom came home to live with her and her husband. This treatment prevents their kids from truly reaching **maturity**.

C Underline an appeal to authority in the first half of the passage.

It's painful to recognize that adults cannot be **reliant** on their parents forever, and that many life lessons must be learned alone. This truth is compounded by baby boomers'[9] refusal to acknowledge getting older, which sends an additional message to young

1 **shove** *n.* a push
2 **apace** *adv.* quickly
3 **mortgage** *n.* a loan to buy a home
4 **realm** *n.* an area of activity, influence, etc.
5 **soothe** *v.* to cause pain to go away; to relieve
6 **tether** *v.* to tie
7 **pampered** *adj.* treated with a lot of attention and care
8 **dormant** *adj.* temporarily inactive
9 **baby boomer** *n.* a member of the "baby boom" generation, the unusually large generation born after World War II

adults that there will always be time to get another degree, to break up with one more partner or employer, or to change direction. If parents aren't "old" (and with hair color and joint replacements, who doesn't want to pretend they're still 40?), then for adultescents, the years must be standing still. Parents of adult children need to step back so young adults can step forward.

Gareth Johnson, 38, lives with his parents and his nephew in south London

Gareth says: "My mum and dad are extremely supportive. They've never brought up the subject of me leaving. I'm unemployed—I got a master's in forensic art[10] a few years ago, but haven't found work in that area yet, even though I've applied for more than 300 jobs.

"Everything changed when my sister died suddenly six years ago. I had been considering moving out and that put a hold on things; it changed my whole perspective on life. I used to work in TV production design, and it made me want to do something more worthwhile, which is why I did my postgraduate degree.

Q Why did Gareth decide to get another degree?

"Mum and Dad are raising my nephew, Seth, and I'm a sort of dad/uncle/brother to him. They provide him with stability, as they do for me. I get unemployment benefits, so I don't pay any rent. We eat together most evenings, but cooking is a bit of a problem: my mum and dad don't eat the sort of stuff I like, so they tend to do the cooking. Dad does most of the cleaning, but I do my own laundry and clean up after dinner. I don't get any teasing from my friends, as they've all done the back-to-home thing before."

Gareth's father, Carl, says: "If we had the money to set him up on his own, we would. Some members of our family think we're a bit too supportive and drop hints that Gareth should try to find a job, but we do like having him around. Like any family member, he has good and bad points: he's always leaving the lights on, but he brews fabulous beer. He and Seth get along wonderfully: they play football in the hall, just like Gareth did as a kid with his own uncles."

Q Who is Seth, and why do you think he lives with Gareth's parents?

Michelle Nicoll, 27, and her husband David, 30, live with her parents in Essex

Michelle says: "David and I had been renting for two years before we got engaged and realized we'd never be able to afford a wedding and a deposit for a house while wasting money on rent. We had no savings; and though we didn't want a big wedding, we wanted all the family there, so our only option was to move back in with my parents.

It was depressing—I felt as if we were imposing, and that we'd failed. The hardest part was adjusting to my parents' routines. When we lived together, we did chores when we felt like it, and now we feel we have to wash up right after dinner, or tidy up when they want us to. Between us, David and I pay £225 a month in rent, which probably doesn't even cover food or utilities."

Michelle's mother, Jan, says: "We thought, if we don't help Michelle and David out, there's no chance of them getting anywhere. Michelle and I are very different, and we have clashed[11], particularly in the kitchen. They have two cats and it took our dog a while to get used to them, and we had to work out timings for the bathroom in the morning, as we have only one. For their sake, mostly, I'm looking forward to when they move out and can get their lives in order."

[10] **forensic art** *n.* the skills practiced by artists in police work, such as drawing suspects' faces

[11] **clash** *v.* to argue; to fight

READING COMPREHENSION

A **Organize the ideas from the reading. Review the passage and fill in the graphic organizer below.**

Generation boomerang

Recent UK trends

- Number of adults living at home up by [1] ________________ since 1997
- Higher tuition leading to [2] ________________
- High unemployment and home prices
- Parents pamper them, so kids not mature

Gareth

- Parents very supportive
- Has applied for hundreds of jobs
- Parents also raising [3] ________________
- Does some chores
- Some relatives think [4] ________________

Michelle

- Married and saving money to buy [5] ________________
- Trouble adjusting to [6] ________________
- Clashes with mother
- Mom can't wait for them to move out

B **Choose the best answer according to the reading.**

1 What can be inferred about baby boomers from paragraph 5?

a. Their parents wish they were more independent.
b. They want to see themselves as young.
c. They were unusually dependent on their parents when young.
d. They are better educated than their children are.

2 Which is NOT true about Michelle Nicoll and her husband?

a. Her parents will be glad when they move out.
b. They hadn't saved up any money before getting married.
c. They wanted a large, expensive wedding.
d. They pay rent to her parents.

SUMMARY

Fill in the blanks with the phrases in the box.

his nephew	married couple	in debt
since 1997	household chores	master's degree

"Adultescents" Increasing	Example: Gareth Johnson	Example: Michelle and David Nicoll
• 20-percent rise in young British adults living with their parents ❶ __________ • Many are unemployed and/or ❷ __________ • Parents treat them like pampered teens, keeping them from maturing	• 38 years old; has a(n) ❸ __________ but is unable to find a job • Parents enjoy having him around; helps take care of ❹ __________	• ❺ __________ living with Michelle's parents • They pay a small amount of rent and do ❻ __________ • Mother looks forward to their moving out

DISCUSSION

A **Read the excerpt from the reading passage.**

Generation Boomerang: Children Who Go Back to Mom and Dad

Many young adults, however, exist in a cloud of overconfidence, with an illusion of endless time. "This is a more entitled generation than their parents' and grandparents'," says William J. Doherty, professor of family social science.

B **Discuss the following questions with your partner or classmates.**

1. Do you agree that today's young generation is overconfident and more entitled than previous ones?
2. In what other ways do you think young people today differ from their parents?

WRITING

Write a short paragraph answering the following question.

Q: Do you think it's a good idea for young adults to live with their parents?

☐ **[Opinion 1]** In many cases, I think it's a good idea for young adults to live with their parents.

☐ **[Opinion 2]** I do not think it's a good idea for young adults to live with their parents.

Example

I do not think it's a good idea for young adults to live with their parents. For one thing, it slows down the process of becoming a mature adult. People are not truly adults until they can support themselves and handle their own problems. Living at home prevents young adults from learning important life lessons. Living together can cause tension between parents and children.

My Paragraph

Unit 8 • Human Relationships

Reading 1 The Problems with Athletes as Role Models

BEFORE YOU READ

Talk about these questions with your classmates.

This online article discusses why professional athletes might not make the best role models. Think of two possible problems with viewing famous athletes as role models. Discuss them with a partner.

VOCABULARY PREVIEW

Match each word in bold with its meaning in the box.

a. special consideration; particular importance
b. a period of ten years
c. a group of people born around the same time
d. having more than one possible meaning
e. significant; relating to a subject in an appropriate way

_____ **1** Many athletes don't put much **emphasis** on education.

_____ **2** Tiger Woods made golf popular with the young **generation**.

_____ **3** Some athletes sign agreements to play for an entire **decade**.

_____ **4** "Just Do It" is an **ambiguous** slogan—what exactly does it mean?

_____ **5** The ad Charles Barkley made in 1993 is still **relevant** today.

The Problems with Athletes as Role Models 15

by Alex Ashe

In 1993, Nike released an advertisement with then-pro basketball player Charles Barkley declaring, "I am not a role model." The ad is so **relevant** today that this line could probably replace the increasingly **ambiguous** "Just Do It" as Nike's slogan.

Nike fired the cyclist Lance Armstrong immediately after his drug use became clear. It proved to be a smart move. His lying, wrongful-defamation[1] lawsuits, and attempted justification of his behavior have overshadowed[2] his cheating. Along with his championships, sponsorships, and dignity[3], Armstrong lost the support of millions of people.

In 2012, an inspiring story hit the news. Sprinter Oscar Pistorius had made history by becoming the first double amputee to compete in the Olympics. Just six months later, he was charged with the murder of his girlfriend, Reeva Steenkamp.

And then there's Tiger Woods's fall from grace. News of the golfer's many affairs turned his world upside down in an instant. By destroying his family life, Woods immediately went from being one of the most marketable athletes of all time to being a pariah[4]. The most shocking part about the scandal was that Woods had enjoyed an immaculate[5] reputation since his start in the 1990s. He was responsible for popularizing golf for both the black community and an entire **generation** of young people worldwide. Woods is now a mere mortal[6]. And his legend continues to fade.

Scandals concerning Tiger Woods's personal life damaged his status as a role model.

Q Name the three athletes cited who were once viewed as role models.

Of course, it's perfectly fine to look up to star athletes for their work on the field. But we need to change our expectations of how athletes should act once the final whistle is blown.

By viewing pro athletes as role models, we set ourselves up for disappointment. There seems to be an increasing trend of inspirational sports stories being revealed as too good to be true.

Why is this? With **decade**-long contracts and huge endorsement[7] deals (worth amounts many people can't even comprehend), pro athletes have never been less able to relate to the average citizen.

Many athletes have gotten to where they are with little to no **emphasis** on academics. Many pro baseball and basketball players have forgone[8] higher education. With the NBA now requiring players to spend a minimum of one year in college, academics are just a

1 **defamation** *n.* the act of harming someone's reputation by saying false or unfair things about the person

2 **overshadow** *v.* to cause to seem less important

3 **dignity** *n.* the quality of being worthy of respect

4 **pariah** *n.* someone hated and rejected by others

5 **immaculate** *adj.* perfect; pure

6 **mere mortal** *phrase* an ordinary person who is unimportant

7 **endorsement** *n.* an agreement by a celebrity to promote a product

8 **forgo** *v.* to give up

front for some players. During the recent college basketball championships, commentator Dick Vitale described the rule as "a mockery[9] of the academic system."

Because they live lives rooted in both luxury and stress, it's difficult for professional athletes to maintain perfectly clean images. With the non-stop media coverage, it's even harder for them to get away with their mistakes.

Who, then, should kids view as role models?

It's ironic that so many sports stars turn out to be false idols when perhaps the most genuine and charitable athlete comes from a business often described as "fake."

Pro wrestling is practically a soap opera, starring live-action superheroes and super-villains. Characters, storylines, and matches are presented with great amounts of silliness, drama, and exaggeration. In rare instances, however, pro wrestling writers put bits of truth and reality into the product. This is the case with John Cena of World Wrestling Entertainment (WWE). Cena is a superhero in the ring—and outside as well.

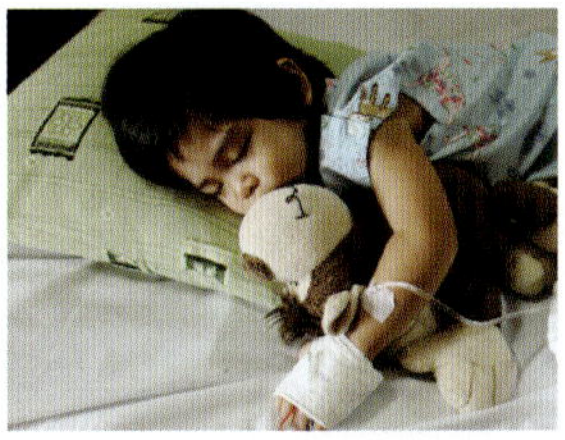

The Make-A-Wish Foundation works to make the wishes of seriously ill children come true.

He is the Make-A-Wish Foundation's all-time leader in wishes granted. He's granted more than three hundred wishes, and hopes to make it to a thousand. As the foundation's most requested wish-granter, Cena has been placed in the role model position for American children. What's refreshing is that he's actually suited for the task of being a positive influence.

The world of wrestling is infamous[10] for steroids and stunts gone wrong. But Cena stands as a symbol of positivity. A champion of "hustle[11], loyalty, and respect," he's served as the face of WWE during its transformation into family-friendly entertainment. Since his 2002 entrance into wrestling, Cena has never played the role of the villain. In other words, he is often written to overcome difficulty and evil, all to show that good things happen to good people.

It's for these exact reasons that Cena draws criticism from the more seasoned wrestling fans. Instead of a respectable role model, they tend to look for edgy[12] characters like Stone Cold Steve Austin or the Rock. But then again, there's a reason why we don't rely on bloodthirsty wrestling fans to determine our role models.

Yes, kids probably need sports role models. But they should be their coaches or someone close who can teach them the difference between right and wrong.

Perhaps Charles Barkley said it best back in 1993.

"Parents should be role models."

Q What is the author's point about athletes and education in this paragraph?

C What is the author's point of view on John Cena?

C What do you think is the author's main purpose in this passage?
(1) To inform
(2) To persuade
(3) To entertain

---

9 **mockery** *n.* a useless or foolish imitation of something

10 **infamous** *adj.* having a bad reputation

11 **hustle** *n.* (*informal*) great effort; good work ethic

12 **edgy** *adj.* tense and irritable

READING COMPREHENSION

Choose the best answer according to the reading.

1 What is the main idea of the passage?

a. Some famous athletes have failed as role models.
b. Children look up to athletes as role models.
c. Athletes must work harder to be good role models.
d. Athletes generally do not make good role models.

2 From paragraph 2, we can infer that the author __________.

a. supports Nike's decision to fire Armstrong
b. admires Armstrong and considers him a role model
c. is unsure whether Armstrong deserved to be fired
d. believes that many people still look up to Armstrong

3 Which is NOT mentioned as a problem with athletes being role models?

a. Their huge salaries
b. Their lack of education
c. Their lack of real talent
d. Their constant media coverage

4 According to the passage, John Cena is a good role model largely because of his __________.

a. family life
b. charity work
c. education
d. determination to win

5 From paragraph 14, what can we infer about John Cena's wrestling career?

a. He plays heroic roles.
b. He has won all of his matches.
c. He has changed a lot since his start in the WWE.
d. He will retire soon.

SUMMARY

Fill in the blanks with the phrases in the box.

his family life	charged with murder	Make-A-Wish Foundation
not well-educated	pro wrestler	media coverage

Disappointing Athlete-Role Models

- Lance Armstrong: caught using drugs and lying
- Oscar Pistorius: ❶ ____________
- Tiger Woods: destroyed ❷ ____________

Why Most Athletes Make Bad Role Models

- Many are extremely wealthy but ❸ ____________
- Combination of luxury, stress, and constant ❹ ____________

John Cena: A Genuine Athlete-Role Model

- A ❺ ____________
- Active at the ❻ ____________; family-friendly
- Shows that good things happen to good people

DISCUSSION

Discuss the following questions with your partner or classmates.

1 Some people argue that famous athletes have a responsibility to behave well because children look up to them. Do you agree or disagree?

2 Besides athletes, what other kinds of people do kids see as role models? Is that good or bad, in your opinion?

WRITING

Write a short paragraph answering the following question.

Q: Who is your most important role model, and why?

☐ **[Opinion]** My most important role model is my mother / my father / my teacher / ____________________.

Example

My most important role model is my mother. She demonstrates humanity, as all role models should. My mother always shows care and compassion, especially in the way she works hard to take care of our entire family. She provides a realistic role model. Unlike famous entertainers or athletes, my mother is a role model that I can relate to and try to imitate. Furthermore, she can give me guidance directly. As someone who knows me closely and whom I communicate with every day, my mother can guide me better than anyone else can. Many people look for role models among the rich and famous, whose lives seem perfect. As scandals in professional sports show, many admired celebrities are anything but perfect. I hope to be like my mother, and I think everyone should look for a role model whom they know personally.

My Paragraph

Unit 8 • Human Relationships

Reading 2 Male and Female Friendships: Shoulder-to-Shoulder vs. Face-to-Face

BEFORE YOU READ

Talk about these questions with your classmates.

1 What do women usually do together as they get to know a new friend? What about men?
2 How do male and female friendships differ?

VOCABULARY PREVIEW

Match each word in bold with its meaning in the box.

a. the act of leaving or taking away support
b. naturally; without thinking
c. increased or built up over time
d. a limit or boundary
e. an event causing great and sudden damage and suffering

_____ **1** Between female friends, loss of trust is a **catastrophe**, both socially and psychologically.

_____ **2** Women build friendships based on the **accumulated** experiences they share.

_____ **3** Males often form friendships within the **parameters** of shared activities.

_____ **4** Among female friends, **abandonment** is the worst crime.

_____ **5** Boys **automatically** build friendships based on playing games together.

Male and Female Friendships:
Shoulder-to-Shoulder vs. Face-to-Face

by Kelly Shepherd / Language Cradle Consulting

Men and women think and feel differently about a myriad[1] of subjects, and this includes the friendships they have. Traditionally, females are seen as being more driven by their feelings, and males are seen as more oriented toward action. Movies and books commonly depict female friendships as centered on sharing emotions, seeking and giving advice, and providing empathy[2]. Their friendships are created and maintained around those activities. Men, however, are put into roles as action figures: they go out and conquer enemies and become heroes with a friend beside them, much like Batman and Robin.

These stories perpetuate[3] stereotypes surrounding how men and women differ, and stereotypes, of course, never express the full complexity of real women and men. However, it can't be denied that they have some basis in reality.

Men's friendships are usually based on sports and other "shoulder-to-shoulder" activities.

From an early age, male friendships are typically built around sports and games, as boys generally love competing against one another. Males seem to **automatically** form friendships through shared activities rather than through shared feelings. In one survey of Americans, eighty percent of men said they participated in sports with their friends. Not a single woman gave that answer. "Men do not easily make revelations of strong emotional responses," Dr. Roger Gould, a psychiatrist, told *Atlantic Monthly*. But doing things together provides an experience of shared accomplishment and recognition. Boys and men learn to support one another within these **parameters**, and this builds bonds between them.

C Underline the appeal to authority in this paragraph.

To use terms coined by psychologist Paul Wright, while men have "shoulder-to-shoulder" friendships, women have "face-to-face" ones. Females also enjoy sharing common experiences; however, their bonding methods are significantly different from those of males. It is more important for females to communicate verbally with one another. Women's studies and education scholar Lyn Mikel Brown asserts that a female's friendships are a "psychological safety net." Women share issues of work, family, and relationships with their friends as common ground for exploring ways to handle tough situations. These **accumulated** experiences are important factors within female's friendships, helping them get through the problems they face.

Q List the similarity and difference between men and women in forming friendships.

1 **myriad** *n.* a very large number

2 **empathy** *n.* shared emotion based on shared or similar experiences

3 **perpetuate** *v.* to cause to continue

Women's friendships tend to form and grow through "face-to-face" experiences.

Bonding is a high priority for both males and females. Yet females seem to place more importance on the loyalty and trust these bonds create than do males. This may be because women develop such intense bonds in their friendships that, when a disagreement comes up, it could have a deeper effect on their lives than it would on men's lives. A loss of trust between female friends is not a matter of a simple disagreement, but more like a psychological and social **catastrophe**.

This is skillfully portrayed in the 2004 movie *Mean Girls*, in which the main character, a girl named Cady, is a newcomer at her high school. She quickly makes friends with the outsider Janis, who warns Cady to stay away from a group of popular but mean girls that have bullied her for years. However, Cady is gradually drawn into the mean girls' social circle and ultimately snubs[4] Janis, who is deeply hurt and angry. The movie earned over $100 million worldwide, so obviously its depiction of female friendships is believable. It gives us a realistic glimpse[5] into female relationships, in which trust is everything, and betrayal and **abandonment** are the worst possible crimes.

In an article titled "The Complicated Business of Female Friendships," the author Elizabeth Gilbert suggests that the ending of female friendships can be "just as painful as any severed[6] romantic relationship." Female friendships are difficult to replace because women invest so much in their friendships. This does not mean that males view the friendships they have as being any less important than females do; the difference is in how they approach the problems that arise within those friendships.

On the website *artofmanliness.com*, a post titled "The History and Nature of Man Friendship" describes the tactics[7] males use when irritated by one another. "When a guy is bothered by something that his friend is doing, he simply tells his friend; they discuss it, sometimes heatedly[8], and then move on." Males don't see a point in brooding[9] over something their friend said or did. They also don't impose their views on their friends if they disagree about something. Males, it seems, would rather get to the bottom of[10] the issue. If they don't see eye to eye, they don't have a problem walking away from the friendship.

Q What do men do when a friend's action bothers them? Underline the information.

To sum up, books and movies aren't entirely wrong: men's and women's friendships are distinct from one another. But in both sexes, they bind people together through shared experiences and accomplishments. Friendships are among our most meaningful relationships, carrying both women and men through their lives in an enriching way.

C Underline the conclusion of this passage.

4 **snub** *v.* to ignore in an insulting way
5 **glimpse** *n.* a look
6 **severed** *adj.* cut off; ended
7 **tactic** *n.* an action meant to achieve a goal
8 **heatedly** *adv.* with excited or angry feelings
9 **brood** *v.* to think anxiously or sadly
10 **get to the bottom of (something)** *idiom* to find an explanation for; to discover the truth about

READING COMPREHENSION

Choose the best answer according to the reading.

1 The author thinks that fictional portrayals of male and female friendships are ___________.

a. completely different from reality
b. accurate about women but not about men
c. based on outdated facts and customs
d. overly simple but partly true

2 What is the main idea of paragraph 3?

a. Boys' friendships are similar to men's.
b. Sports are more important to men than to women.
c. Male bonding centers on shared activities.
d. Both boys and men enjoy competition.

3 Why does the author discuss the movie *Mean Girls*?

a. To illustrate a point about how much women value trust
b. To give an example of a wrong depiction of female friendship
c. To help explain why women's friendships have more conflict
d. To argue that female friends are more likely to betray each other

4 What can be inferred from paragraph 7?

a. A man and woman who were romantically involved cannot be friends anymore.
b. Men tend to be less deeply affected by the loss of a friendship.
c. When women lose a female friendship, they do not try to replace it.
d. Women find it harder to have both close friends and a romantic relationship.

5 Which of the following is true, according to paragraph 8?

a. When men are irritated with a friend, they usually don't say anything.
b. Men usually insist that their friends agree with them.
c. Men are quite likely to brood over a conflict with a friend.
d. It's fairly easy for a man to end a friendship.

SUMMARY

Fill in the blanks with the phrases in the box.

move on	sharing feelings	helping each other
verbal communication	trust and loyalty	shared activities

Males

- Base friendships on ❶ ________________ such as sports and games
- Build bonds "shoulder-to-shoulder" rather than by ❷ ________________
- Usually discuss a conflict and then ❸ ________________

Females

- Base friendships on ❹ ________________
- Build bonds "face-to-face" by sharing and ❺ ________________ with problems
- Value ❻ ________________ more intensely, as portrayed in the movie *Mean Girls*

DISCUSSION

Discuss the following questions with your partner or classmates.

1. What is a movie or book that you think presents male or female friendships in a believable way?
2. Think about your own experiences with (male or female) friendships. Are they similar to the descriptions in the reading?

WRITING

Write a short paragraph answering the following question.

Q: What are the main differences between male and female friendships?

☐ **[Opinion]** Male and female friendships differ in three main ways: what friends do together, ____________________, and ____________________.

Example

Male and female friendships differ in three main ways: what friends do together, what they talk about, and how they deal with conflict. Females tend to bond "face-to-face" while males tend to bond "shoulder-to-shoulder." Women make friends by talking while men make friends by doing things together. Another difference is in what women and men talk about with their friends. It's important to women to share their feelings and give each other empathy. Men are much less likely to talk about their feelings. Men and women react differently when a friend lets them down. Women are more deeply affected because their friendships are more emotionally intense. Men seem to get over conflicts faster and find it easier to end a friendship. It might appear that males do not value friendship as much as females do. However, it is more accurate to say that males and females just have different styles of friendship because studies show that boys' friendships last just as long as girls' and are as satisfying. Despite these differences, people of both sexes value and benefit from their friendships.

My Paragraph

Unit 9 • Ethics

Reading 1 Should You Give Money to Homeless People?

BEFORE YOU READ

Talk about these questions with your classmates.

1 Is giving money directly to beggars the best way to solve the problem of homelessness?
2 Can you think of three reasons why giving money to the homeless might not be the best way to help them?

Think About It

What is the best way of helping those in need?

VOCABULARY PREVIEW

Choose the one that is closest to the meaning of the word in bold.

1 Because people are responding to questions about personal drug or alcohol use, there is probably self-reported **bias**.
a. preference b. problem c. presentation

2 The **income** of a homeless person from begging is usually between $600 and $1,500 a month.
a. spending b. money earned c. waste

3 Altruism is a major **factor** influencing people to give money to the homeless as it makes us feel good.
a. game b. authority c. reason

4 The government stated **explicitly** that the most efficient way to improve the economy is to give money to the poor.
a. slowly b. clearly c. recently

5 The economist Tyler Cowen is **consistently** interesting and funny.
a. extremely b. always c. rarely

Should You Give Money to Homeless People? 17

by Derek Thompson

Q What are the two sides of giving money to the homeless that the author refers to here? Circle them.

Giving money to the homeless is an economic crisis of the heart. It involves a tug-of-war between the instinct to alleviate[1] suffering and the knowledge that a donation might actually encourage the anguish[2] of the poor.

We're all familiar with our mothers' reasons not to empty our pockets for beggars*. "The best help is a shelter, not a dollar," she's told us. "They'll only use it on [something bad] anyway!"

C What evidence does the author give that homeless people are likely to use the money they receive to buy drugs and alcohol? Underline it.

Sixty percent of the homeless report having problems with drugs or alcohol.

The studies seem to back up mom, to a degree. One report from the Department of Housing and Urban Development found that six out of ten homeless respondents admitted problems with alcohol or drugs. Given the likelihood of self-reported **bias**, the actual number could be even higher. Studies on homeless **income** find that the typical "career panhandler" who dedicates[3] his time overwhelmingly to begging can make between $600 and $1,500 a month. But since panhandlers often have no way to save their money, they have a good reason to spend most of their day's earnings quickly. This creates a tendency to spend on short-term relief, rather than long-term needs, which can feed this dependency on alcoholic relief.

The Case for Giving

Q Why do economists think that giving money to the homeless is an efficient way of helping them? Circle two reasons.

What do economists say about the instinct to help the homeless? (For these purposes, I'm ignoring the altruism[4] **factor**, the idea that if giving 50 cents makes us feel good then it's an inherently justifiable donation.) Some argue that giving cash to cash-needy people is the most efficient way to spend it. Indeed, the Congressional Budget Office has stated **explicitly** that the most efficient government stimulus[5] targets the poorest Americans. And who's poorer than a homeless person? What's more, if you donate to a charity, there are administrative costs and time lags. If you put your money in the hands of a beggar, however, it's fast, easy, and guaranteed to be spent immediately.

Q What does the author mean by "strings attached"?

But the fact that beggars are likely to spend their money quickly is also the problem. Food stamps are considered highly effective government spending. But they're earmarked[6] for food. Unemployment benefits can go a long way. But recipients have to prove that they're looking for work. A dollar from your hand to a homeless person's has no such strings attached.

1 **alleviate** *v.* to make better; to ease
2 **anguish** *n.* mental pain; suffering
3 **dedicate** *v.* to give one's time or energy to something
4 **altruism** *n.* unselfishness; selflessness
5 **stimulus** *n.* an action taken to improve the economy
6 **earmark** *v.* to reserve something for a purpose

But what would happen if we provided both money and strings? *Good* magazine found a British non-profit that identified 15 long-term homeless people, asked what they needed to change their lives, and just bought it for them. Some asked for items as simple as shoes, or cash to repay a loan. One asked for a camper van. All were given 3,000 pounds and a "broker" to help them manage their budget. Of the 13 who agreed to take part, 11 were off the street within a year, and several entered treatment for addiction[7].

The lesson: The homeless often need something more than money. They need money and direction. For most homeless people, direction means a job and a roof. A 1999 study from HUD asked homeless people what they needed most: 42 percent said help finding a job; 38 percent said finding housing; 30 percent said paying rent or utilities; 13 percent said training or medical care.

C A non-profit gave money, items, and advice to the homeless. In your own words, what is the author's point of view on this?

But What Should You Do?

Organizations can do more for the needy than we can with the change in our back pocket. But does that mean we shouldn't give, ever?

The **consistently** entertaining economist Tyler Cowen worries that giving to beggars induces bad long-term incentives. If you travel to a poor city, for example, you'll find lots of beggars by touristy locations. If the tourists become more generous, the local beggars don't get richer. They only multiply. Generous people attract more beggars. Cowen writes:

Q What is a likely effect of giving beggars money? Circle the effect.

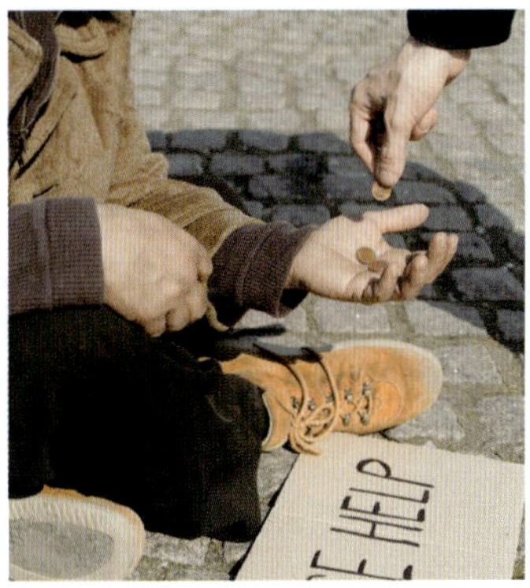

This might not be the best way to help the homeless.

"The more you give to beggars, the harder beggars will try. This leads to what economists call 'rent exhaustion,' which again limits the net gain to beggars . . . If you are going to give, pick the poor person who is expecting it least."

I'm certain that there are some cases in which donations to an especially needy beggar are justified. But the ultimate danger in panhandling is that we don't give to every beggar. There's not enough change in our purses. We choose to donate money based on the level of perceived need. Beggars know this, so there is an incentive on their part to exaggerate[8] their need, by either lying about their circumstances or letting their appearance visibly deteriorate rather than seek help.

If we drop change in a beggar's hand without donating to a charity, we're acting to relieve our guilt rather than the underlying crisis of poverty. The same thing applies to the beggar who relies on begging for alcohol. In short, both sides fail each other by being lured[9] into a fleeting[10] sense of relief rather than a lasting solution to the problem of homelessness.

Q Does the author support or oppose individuals' giving money directly to beggars? Underline the sentence that best shows his opinion.

* Academic research, journalism articles, and everyday conversation often use the words *homeless*, *beggar*, and *panhandler* to describe the same group. But if we're being precise, not all homeless people are beggars, and not all beggars are homeless.

7 **addiction** *n.* dependency on drugs or alcohol
8 **exaggerate** *v.* to overstate
9 **lure** *v.* to attract
10 **fleeting** *adj.* lasting a short time

READING COMPREHENSION

A **Organize the ideas from the reading. Review the passage and fill in the graphic organizer below.**

Should we give money directly to the homeless?

Reasons not to give money:

- Money is spent on [1] ____________ or drugs
- Attracts more beggars to area
- Beggars [2] ____________ situation to appear needier
- Only relieves our [3] ____________—doesn't solve problem

Reasons to give money:

- Most [4] ____________ way to help needy
- All the money goes directly to homeless

Answer:

- Give money through [5] ____________

B **Choose the best answer according to the reading.**

1 According to the article, which is NOT true of the homeless?

a. Most of them have drug or alcohol problems.
b. Many of them spend their money quickly.
c. They often seek long-term relief to their problems.
d. They sometimes make a career out of begging.

2 What is true of food stamps according to the author?

a. They must be used for food.
b. They are easy to give out.
c. They target just the unemployed.
d. They're only used for people who look for work.

SUMMARY

Write the number of each sentence under the category it belongs to.

Giving to the Homeless	
Reasons to Give	Reasons Not to Give

1. When tourists are generous to beggars, touristy areas attract more beggars.
2. Research suggests that more than half of homeless people have drug or alcohol problems.
3. A direct donation to a homeless person is quick and efficient, with no administrative costs.
4. Since the homeless have no way to save their money, they spend it quickly.
5. Donations help if they are used to buy something useful or if they come with assistance in making a budget.
6. People give money according to perceived need, so beggars exaggerate how needy they are.

DISCUSSION

A Read the excerpt from the reading passage.

Should You Give Money to Homeless People?

If we drop change in a beggar's hand without donating to a charity, we're acting to relieve our guilt rather than the underlying crisis of poverty. The same thing applies to the beggar who relies on begging for alcohol. In short, both sides fail each other by being lured into a fleeting sense of relief rather than a lasting solution to the problem of homelessness.

B Talk with a partner about a time when you gave money to a homeless person or a charity.

1 How did you give?
2 How did it feel to give the money?
3 Do you think the money helped the person who received it?

WRITING

Write a short paragraph answering the following question.

Q: Would you give money to the homeless?

☐ **[Opinion 1]** No, I would not give money to the homeless.

☐ **[Opinion 2]** Yes, I would give money to the homeless.

Example

I would not give money to the homeless. It's been argued that giving money to the homeless can solve the problem. Unfortunately, this is not the case in reality. The homeless are very likely to spend the money on drugs or alcohol. In a recent poll taken by the US Department of Housing and Urban Development, sixty percent of the homeless admitted to having drug or alcohol problems. So if you give them money, it will do them more harm. The real problem of the homeless is that they lack the life skills needed to function in society. These people don't always know how to find employment, shelter, or even medical care. They need the professional help of charitable organizations to overcome these problems. Giving just money to the homeless won't solve anything. The homeless need not only money but also guidance.

My Paragraph

Unit 9 • Ethics

Reading 2 How Tracking Customers In-store Will Soon Be the Norm

BEFORE YOU READ

Talk about these questions with your classmates.

Do you think it is OK for governments to listen to people's phone calls and read their emails? If yes, in what situations? If no, why not? Make a list of reasons and share it with a partner.

Think About It

Do you feel safe knowing that companies and other organizations collect information about you?

VOCABULARY PREVIEW

Match each word in bold with its meaning in the box.

a. a set of rules or guidelines related to behavior or activity in a particular area
b. hesitant and unwilling to do something
c. to put a decision, plan, agreement, etc. into effect
d. to gather together to form a whole
e. new; just recently becoming known

_____ **1** Companies will be able to **implement** the system at their stores for free.

_____ **2** Now there is no reason for **reluctant** businesses not to use it.

_____ **3** A **code** of conduct was launched to control how companies use customer information.

_____ **4** At this time, the company is only able to give **aggregate** information.

_____ **5** The obvious goal of this **emerging** technology is to identify individual customers.

How Tracking Customers In-store Will Soon Be the Norm

18

by Siraj Datoo

At the Fairson's department store, managers can measure the number of people who walk past the store and the number who come through the front door. Also, this information includes whether or not these people come in immediately or are convinced to do so by the shop front.

Once shoppers are inside the store, managers can find out how many of them walk up to the second floor and compare that with the number of people who took the journey to the second floor last week. If more people have gone up this week, managers will probably conclude that the marketing banners put up toward the beginning of the week are working.

Q What is Euclid's strategy for getting more retailers to use its technology? Underline it.

In this scenario, Fairson's is imaginary. But this technology is very real. Euclid, a California-based analytics[1] company, is hoping to gain wider acceptance of tracking technology by offering its Euclid Express for free to all retailers[2]. This means that, at no cost, stores will be able to **implement** an analytics package to receive information that could help guide their marketing.

Why is Euclid offering its services at no cost to clients? One reason is competition. Euclid's is currently the only offline customer analytics platform that is available for free. This provides the company with a strong competitive advantage over rivals such as ShopperTrak and Prism Skylabs. Moreover, Euclid wants to lower the barriers[3] to entry so there is no longer any reason for **reluctant** businesses not to implement this technology.

Stores can collect information through customers' smart phones.

Late in 2012, Euclid released its next product, called Euclid Zero. Eliminating the need for companies to install sensors[4] in their stores, Euclid Zero connects retailers to a cloud-based analytics service using Wi-Fi. Businesses then collect information about customer behavior by monitoring the media access code (MAC) in every smart phone that enters the store.

Q Euclid gives three responses to concerns about its technology. What are they? Underline them.

Euclid Zero has received a lot of criticism from consumers concerned about their privacy being violated[5]. But Euclid assures that the MAC data is scrambled[6], which means that no personally identifiable information is collected. Second, they point to the fact that Euclid is a part of the group that launched the Mobile Location Analytics **code** of conduct[7]. These sets of rules require companies to receive customers' consent before they can collect any

1 **analytics** *n.* the logical analysis of data and statistics

2 **retailer** *n.* a person or business that sells goods directly to the public

3 **barrier** *n.* something that is blocking or preventing a process

4 **sensor** *n.* a device that detects and responds to certain changes in the environment

5 **violate** *v.* to not respect someone's right to something

6 **scramble** *v.* to mix up a signal or message so that it cannot be understood

7 **conduct** *n.* the way a person acts; behavior

personal information. Euclid also helped found a central opt-out[8] site for consumers. This site was praised by the Federal Trade Commission for "recognising consumer concerns about invisible tracking in retail spaces and taking a positive step forward in developing a code of conduct."

But it's worth noting that the code of conduct most likely was signed following complaints from angry customers when they found out that they were being monitored. For instance, American department store Nordstrom put up a sign in May 2013 that announced it had been using the technology for months. Subsequently, it received a number of complaints made directly to its store and also on social media.

C What inference does the author make about the reason why the code of conduct was created?

The potential for the technology also means that it could upset many. "I would think permission would need to be given to use something that belongs to someone else. Even if it is just a signal," one consumer posted on Facebook.

Another example is that of a marketing startup company named Renew in Britain. It tracked pedestrians in the City of London through their smart phones using devices hidden in recycling bins. Renew claimed that people could opt out if they so desire, but privacy supporters questioned the idea of people opting out of something they didn't know was taking place.

Renew planned on using the data it was compiling to provide shoppers with personalised advertising on their digital screens. "Why not Pret?" is a message that might be displayed to a regular visitor of Starbucks, the main competitor of café Pret a Manger. Over time, Renew could also tell whether consumers have altered their habits.

But Renew's CEO was adamant[9] that this was not personal information. "As long as we don't add a name and home address, it's legal," he said.

This adds a new element[10] to the conversation. As it stands, Euclid provides only **aggregate** information. But there is potential for more personalised marketing. For instance, a coffee drinker visiting a store might see a message informing him or her of a coffee shop on the second floor. Although the company would not know whom exactly it was marketing to, it would still understand the person's shopping habits.

Q What example of personalised marketing does the author give in this paragraph?

Emma Carr, a senior director at Big Brother Watch, believes that this technology ignores customers' privacy. "This is a clear example of profit trumping[11] privacy," she said. "The use of surveillance technology by shops in order to provide a better or more personalised service seems totally disproportionate[12]."

Carr also stressed the importance of consumer awareness. She said that while the **emerging** technology was still developing, there was an obvious goal in mind to identify individuals. Companies like Euclid won't stop at general information like the length of time that customers spend in stores. The long game is about identifying individuals, and this technology is very close to enabling Euclid to do that.

"It is not only essential that customers are fully informed if they are being monitored, but that they also have real choice of service and on what terms it is offered."

This type of personalised *Minority Report*-style marketing has sparked a new debate: Is your MAC your personal information?

8 **opt-out** *n.* a decision not to participate

9 **adamant** *adj.* determined not to change one's decision or opinion

10 **element** *n.* a basic part of something

11 **trump** *v.* to surpass or outdo

12 **disproportionate** *adj.* out of proportion, as in quantity or appearance; unbalanced

READING COMPREHENSION

A **Organize the ideas from the reading. Review the passage and fill in the graphic organizer below.**

Customer tracking systems

System	• Euclid Express offered [1] ________________ to help guide marketing • Euclid Zero connects retailers to [2] ________________ to monitor customers' smartphones	• Renew tracked people in London using [6] ________________ to provide personalized advertising
Fears	• Customers worry their [3] ________________ and that their MAC data is in danger	• Customers could opt out, but they [7] ________________
Justification	• Euclid says MAC data is [4] ________________ • Also formed a [5] ________________ that requires users' consent to collect info	• No [8] ________________ included, so customers' identities remain private

B **Choose the best answer according to the reading.**

1 All of the following are ways that Euclid protects consumers' privacy EXCEPT:

a. They operate a website where consumers can opt out of being monitored
b. They created a privacy code of conduct that other companies also follow
c. They scramble the personal information that their technology collects
d. They report retailers that do not protect people's personal information

2 According to the reading passage, which statement would Emily Carr agree with?

a. Personalized marketing is a trend that retailers and consumers should embrace.
b. Companies will move away from collecting only general information to data that identifies people.
c. People can trust the government to make sure companies do not invade their privacy.
d. All advertisements should be clearly marked and displayed where customers can see them.

SUMMARY

Fill in the blanks with the phrases in the box.

personalized ads	keep track of	gaining acceptance
privacy concerns	stay fully informed	personal information

Imagine a method by which store managers could continually ❶ ________________ how many people walk by their store and how many enter it, thus determining how effective their marketing is. A company called Euclid is offering such services for free to retailers in the hope of ❷ ________________ for tracking technology. One of Euclid's products uses the media access code (MAC) in customers' smart phones in order to track them, which has led to ❸ ________________ and complaints from many consumers. Another company used hidden sensors to track pedestrians' smart phones in London, using the data to provide shoppers with ❹ ________________. These companies insist that they do not collect ❺ ________________ and that consumers can opt out. However, one expert warns that identifying individuals is the next step for this technology, and that it is important for consumers to ❻ ________________.

DISCUSSION

A **Read the excerpt from the reading passage.**

How Tracking Customers In-store Will Soon Be the Norm

For instance, American department store Nordstrom put up a sign in May 2013 that announced it had been using the technology for months. Subsequently, it received a number of complaints made directly to its store and also on social media.

B **Discuss the following questions with your partner or classmates.**

1 How would you feel if a store you shopped at regularly had been monitoring your shopping behavior without your knowing?

2 How would you respond in this situation?

WRITING

Write a short paragraph answering the following question.

Q: Is it OK for companies and other organizations to collect information about people?

☐ **[Opinion 1]** More often than not, I believe that it is OK for companies and other organizations to collect people's information, as long as they do not abuse its use.

☐ **[Opinion 2]** I am strongly opposed to the collection of people's information by companies and businesses. Privacy is very important to me, with the priority always being protection from intrusive marketing practices, ____________, and ____________.

Example

I am strongly opposed to the collection of personal information by businesses and other organizations because of the potential for abuse and crime. When companies have information about individual consumers, they will bombard people with personalized ads. Unsolicited ads clutter inboxes and annoy the recipients. I believe most people would look for a product or service in a store or online when they need it; they don't simply buy something that is advertised. Criminals hacking into networked systems to steal personal information is a real danger. There are many cases of identity theft in which criminals steal people's bank information and then take all the money in their accounts. Allowing the government to collect citizens' private information risks abuses.

My Paragraph

Unit 10 • Language & Literature

Reading 1 Ever-Evolving English

BEFORE YOU READ

Talk about these questions with your classmates.

1 Which languages have influenced the development of your native language?
2 Do you know any languages that have influenced the development of English?

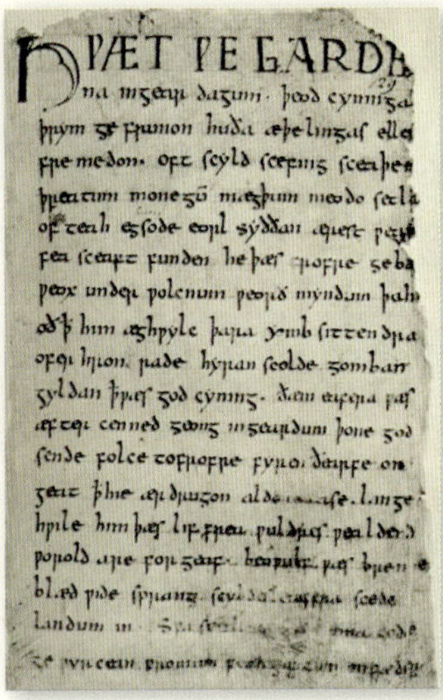

VOCABULARY PREVIEW

Fill in the blanks with the words in the box. Change the form of the word if necessary.

consensus	profound	pronounce	standardize	vowel

1 The Norman invasion had a(n) ________________ impact on English culture.

2 One difference between British and American English is that British English speakers do not ________________ the "r" in words such as "hard."

3 The names of some Welsh towns look unusual because they have no ________________, such as Bwlch in southern Wales.

4 Many tribal languages are almost impossible to ________________ because they have no writing systems.

5 The ________________ of film critics seems to be that the movie is well worth seeing.

Ever-Evolving English 19

Like all languages, English has undergone many fundamental changes over time. The first form of English, now referred to as Old English (OE) or Anglo-Saxon, was first spoken in England and parts of Scotland. It was spoken between the middle of the fifth and twelfth centuries and was characterized by a comparatively limited vocabulary, as well as numerous endings that marked the gender, number, and case[1] of words.

When the Normans invaded the British Isles in 1066, English came under the influence of the French-speaking conquerors[2], who became the new aristocracy[3]. The class differences of this period are still reflected in the language. The words "beef," "pork," and "poultry," for instance, all come from French, yet the words "cow," "pig," and "chicken" all have OE origins. This reveals who was taking care of these expensive animals and who was eating them: as one popular saying puts it, "French for the table, English for the stable." Besides adding many French words, the language also gradually lost many of its OE endings. This new form of English, referred to as Middle English (ME), developed from 1066 to around 1500.

Q Circle the date when French speakers invaded England.

Meanwhile, between 1200 and 1600, a major alteration occurred in the way people **pronounced** many **vowel** sounds, particularly the long vowels. The completion of this change, dubbed[4] "the Great Vowel Shift," marks the birth of the modern English language. Modern English developed rapidly during the reign of Elizabeth I (1558-1603), which was also the period when the great playwright William Shakespeare lived and wrote. His work had a **profound** influence on the language, introducing many new words and phrases that we now take for granted—like "uncomfortable," which comes from *Romeo and Juliet*.

Modern English was characterized by more active attempts at standardization of English usage[5] and spelling. During the 1600s and 1700s, many writers called for English to follow more regular patterns, as French and Latin did. They also proposed that an English academy be created. No such academy was ever established, but numerous grammar texts and dictionaries started appearing.

Q What two languages influenced efforts to standardize English?

Shakespeare may have coined as many as 1,700 new words.

The first official book of grammar rules was written by William Loughton in 1734, and in 1761 Joseph Priestley wrote and published *The Rudiments*[6] *of English Grammar*. These texts were based on what the writers considered "correct" grammar rather than on an analysis of how people actually

1 **case** *n.* a form of a noun, pronoun, or adjective indicating its grammatical function in a sentence
2 **conqueror** *n.* one who gains territory by force
3 **aristocracy** *n.* a governing body or upper class usually made up of a hereditary nobility
4 **dub** *v.* to name
5 **usage** *n.* the way in which words and phrases are used in a language community
6 **rudiments** *n.* first principles; basics

spoke and wrote; thus, their approach is referred to as prescriptive[7] grammar. In later years, linguists[8] argued that grammar should describe how people really use language and not how writers think it should be used, adopting an approach called descriptive grammar.

Dictionary makers try to keep up with the ever-changing language.

Today, English is spoken by so many people in so many different countries across the globe that it has become even harder to **standardize**. The contemporary **consensus** lies somewhere between the prescriptive and descriptive approaches. Educators generally try to follow something called Standard English (SE), so as to avoid a complete lack of order in the use of English. However, as one can see in the differences in spelling and vocabulary between, say, British and American English, rules can be difficult to enforce. Think of examples such as the American spelling of words like "organization" or "color," which are spelled "organisation" and "colour" in the UK. Both forms are seen as correct, as long as they are used in the right country.

Q Underline the reason that English is so difficult to standardize today.

To help ensure that Standard English stays up to date, respected dictionaries publish annual lists of new words that have been accepted into the lexicon[9]. These may be words that started out as slang, and many are new technological terms: in 2014 the popular *Merriam-Webster Collegiate Dictionary* added "selfie" and "hashtag."

There have also been some significant changes in grammar over the years. For decades, prescriptivists argued that English sentences should never end in prepositions and that splitting infinitives was incorrect. (An example of a split infinitive is "to really want" instead of "really to want.") These days such rules are generally considered invalid because they come from Latin, which is no longer viewed as a model for English. Correct English grammar is now considered largely a question of functionality, style, and taste; and the context in which language functions is taken into account before passing judgment.

As long as people are able to communicate effectively and have a basic standard to guide them, English serves its linguistic purpose. After all, the only languages not in flux[10] are those that are no longer in use.

7	**prescriptive**	*adj.* giving exact rules or instructions about how something should be done
8	**linguist**	*n.* a person who studies language in a scientific way
9	**lexicon**	*n.* the vocabulary of a particular language
10	**flux**	*n.* a state of flow and change

READING COMPREHENSION

A **Mark each statement as true (*T*) or false (*F*) according to the reading.**

1 ______ The development of Middle English (ME) began when the Normans conquered England.
2 ______ "The Great Vowel Shift" was very significant in the development of Modern English.
3 ______ During the 17th century, an academy for English was established.
4 ______ Priestley was one of three authors of *The Rudiments of English Grammar*.
5 ______ Educators today use a purely descriptive approach to grammar.

B **Choose the best answer according to the reading.**

1 What is the reading mainly about?
   a. Shakespeare's influence on the development of English
   b. The way class differences control how we use language today
   c. The history and development of the English language
   d. The relationship between British history and English development

2 Which of the following best describes prescriptive grammar?
   a. Grammar that is based on what writers considered to be correct
   b. Grammar that describes how people really use language
   c. Grammar that is considered largely a question of style and personal taste
   d. Grammar that has been borrowed from another language

3 What is the main idea of paragraph 5?
   a. There is no longer any single "correct" form of English.
   b. Different acceptable spellings prove spelling is no longer important.
   c. The expansion of British colonies made standardization more important.
   d. Because there are different forms, there is no such thing as improper English.

4 Which is an example of a grammar rule that has recently been relaxed?
   a. Don't end a sentence with a subject.
   b. Don't split infinitives.
   c. Don't begin a sentence with a preposition.
   d. Don't leave out the verb.

SUMMARY

Fill in the blanks with the phrases in the box.

at standardization	limited vocabulary	the Great Vowel Shift
Norman invasion	French influence	relaxed grammar rules

Origins (OE)	Normans (ME)	Modern English	Contemporary English
• Anglo-Saxon had many endings and a(n) ❶ ________. • The period ended with the ❷ ________ in 1066.	• ME was characterized by its ❸ ________. • Class differences made their way into the language.	• Owes much of its development to ❹ ________ • Shakespeare made important contributions to the language. • Marked the first attempts ❺ ________	• English is now a global language with no universally accepted set of standards. • The language continues to evolve, as reflected in new vocabulary and ❻ ________.

DISCUSSION

Discuss the following questions with your partner or classmates.

1 Do you think people should try hard to use "correct" language at all times?

2 Has there ever been an academy set up to establish rules of your language? Do you support the work of such academies?

WRITING

Write a short paragraph answering the following question.

Q: Is it necessary to standardize a language? How about standardization of your language? What do you think?

☐ [Opinion 1] Standardization of my language is important.

☐ [Opinion 2] Standardization of my language is not important.

Example

Standardization of my language is not important. People communicate with each other quite easily without strict rules. In addition, there are millions of people here and they live in different parts of the country. Because people speak a little differently based on where they live, it would be very difficult to standardize our language.

My Paragraph

Reading 2 Manchester's Sherlock Holmes

BEFORE YOU READ

Talk about these questions with your classmates.

1 Do you like detective stories? Why or why not?
2 Have you read any Sherlock Holmes short stories or novels? If so, what did you think?

VOCABULARY PREVIEW

Fill in the blanks with the words in the box. Change the form of the word if necessary.

accent	clever	candidate	correlation	surgeon

1 The different regional ________________ that people have can tell you which part of the country they are from.

2 The ________________ says that her hands are her most important tool.

3 Comedians often have to come up with ________________ responses to people who heckle them from the audience.

4 A(n) ________________ between a health problem and a certain product does not prove the product is causing the problem.

5 Although there are ten qualified ________________, there are only five jobs available.

Manchester's Sherlock Holmes

20

Outside 221b Baker Street, London, a plaque[1] proclaims Sherlock Holmes once lived there. According to local lore, many foreign tourists visit the site—which happens to be the Sherlock Holmes Museum—apparently unaware the world's most famous Briton is a fictional character.

In fact, there was no such address when Sir Arthur Conan Doyle wrote his detective stories. (It was added when Baker Street was extended in the 1930s.) And accounts of droves of adoring but supposedly ignorant fans are also suspect. But such stories—and the canon of Holmes fiction that expands to this day—speak to the allure of the character. Now, one author claims, there is evidence Doyle based Holmes on a real police detective: Jerome Caminada, known in his own time as "the Sherlock Holmes of Manchester."

Angela Buckley is the author of the 2014 book *The Real Sherlock Holmes: The Hidden Story of Jerome Caminada*. In it she examines Manchester detective Caminada's autobiography and Doyle's work to draw comparisons between the real detective—active around the time Doyle created Holmes—and the fictional sleuth[2]. "There are so many parallels," she concludes, "that it is clear Doyle was using parts of this real character for his." Chief among these similarities, Buckley asserts, is intellect[3]. Doyle's fiction hinged on Holmes' almost superhuman powers of deductive reasoning and observation. Caminada, Buckley reports, could identify a career criminal by his walk and had an "encyclopedic knowledge" of the criminal underworld.

Q Underline the main similarity between Holmes and Caminada.

As with Holmes, Caminada was a master of disguise. Holmes goes undercover in many stories, as an Italian priest, a sailor, and an opium addict, among many examples. On real cases, Caminada dressed as a drunkard, a laborer, and even an upper-class professional, imitating the **accents** of each in order to gather information and apprehend suspects.

The BBC TV series *Sherlock* is set in the present day.

Buckley goes on to draw parallels between Caminada's real cases and the fictional capers Holmes solves. Like Holmes, she explains, Caminada apprehended an alluring femme fatale and had a brilliant arch-nemesis. The two were also formidable[4] fighters in spite of their modest stature[5].

1	**plaque**	*n.* a flat, thin piece of wood or metal with writing on it used as a reminder of something such as a historic event
2	**sleuth**	*n.* a detective
3	**intellect**	*n.* the power of rational or intelligent thought
4	**formidable**	*adj.* very powerful or strong; deserving respect
5	**stature**	*n.* height

Is the case closed? Did Doyle in fact base Holmes on Caminada? Going straight to the source, Doyle very clearly identified the medical professor Dr. Joseph Bell as his inspiration for Holmes. Bell was renowned[6] for his keen powers of reasoning in medical diagnoses. Doyle biographers have also suggested development of the character may have been influenced by Sir Henry Littlejohn, an acquaintance who was a forensic **surgeon** with intimate knowledge of hundreds of crime investigations.

221b Baker Street

Q Circle the names of two other men that might have inspired the character of Holmes.

Much of Buckley's premise rests on timing. Caminada had risen to national prominence, she argues, when Doyle was developing Sherlock Holmes. But so had other detectives, such as Leicester's Francis "Tanky" Smith, also known for **clever** disguises and for his vast knowledge of the criminal world. Even if there were only one **candidate** who fit the bill[7], this leaves the question of why Doyle would not credit a detective who inspired him, despite being perfectly willing to credit a physician.

Furthermore, most of Buckley's work is based on unverified[8] accounts from Jerome Caminada's autobiography, published fifteen years after the first appearance of Sherlock Holmes. One reviewer has pointed out some contemporary police detectives resented Doyle's portrayals of them as mediocre[9]. Did Caminada use his book to show that real police were better than that? We cannot be sure, but it is safe to say he had clear motives to present himself in a flattering light.

Q What did some police officers resent about Sherlock Holmes stories?

Which brings us to the modern author and, apparently, the only proponent of the Caminada theory. Although she bills herself as a "family historian," Buckley is in fact a genealogist[10] and has no academic background in history. She may be faulted for failing to verify claims from a single source—an autobiography at that—and for basing her claims on loose **correlations**. But no one can prove she is wrong, either. The question may be destined to remain a mystery.

6	**renowned**	*adj.* famous
7	**fit the bill**	*idiom* to have the required characteristics
8	**unverified**	*adj.* not proven or checked for accuracy
9	**mediocre**	*adj.* not very good
10	**genealogist**	*n.* a person who traces or studies the descent of persons or families

READING COMPREHENSION

A Mark each statement as true (*T*) or false (*F*) according to the reading.

1 ______ Sherlock Holmes actually lived in the building at 221b Baker Street.
2 ______ Sir Arthur Conan Doyle and Jerome Caminada were real-life rivals.
3 ______ Buckley's book identifies Caminada as a highly intelligent man.
4 ______ Sherlock Holmes once pretended to be a priest.
5 ______ It is impossible for Doyle to have based any aspect of Holmes on Caminada.

B Choose the best answer according to the reading.

1 What is the reading mainly about?
   a. The remarkable career of detective Jerome Caminada
   b. An evaluation of the central claims in Angela Buckley's book
   c. The uncanny similarities between a real and a fictional detective
   d. A summary of Sir Arthur Conan Doyle's Sherlock Holmes stories

2 The word apprehend in paragraph 4 is closest in meaning to ______.
   a. understand
   b. notice
   c. escape
   d. catch

3 The phrase the two in paragraph 5 refers to ______.
   a. Buckley and Doyle
   b. Holmes and Caminada
   c. Holmes and his nemesis
   d. Caminada and his femme fatale

4 Which of the following is NOT stated about Angela Buckley?
   a. She is not a real historian.
   b. She is wrong about Jerome Caminada.
   c. She is the sole advocate of the Caminada theory.
   d. She has made claims based on one source.

SUMMARY

Fill in the blanks with the phrases in the box.

disguises himself	knew a surgeon	a genealogist
formidable opponents	deductive reasoning	unverified accounts

Caminada Inspiration Theory	Critique of the Theory
Both Holmes and Caminada had strong powers of ❶ __________ and knowledge of criminals.	Doyle identified Dr. Joseph Bell as his inspiration and ❹ __________ with encyclopedic knowledge.
Holmes ❷ __________ to catch criminals, as did Caminada.	Buckley used ❺ __________ from an autobiography.
Both men had dealings with ❸ __________.	Buckley is ❻ __________ rather than a historian.

DISCUSSION

Discuss the following questions with your partner or classmates.

1. Why do you think Sherlock Holmes is such a popular character? How are police and/or private detectives viewed in your country?
2. Who are the most famous fictional characters in your culture? Do you know whether these characters are based on real people?

WRITING

Write a short paragraph answering the following questions.

1. What do you see as being the primary role of police?
2. List four things the police do for people in your country.
3. What criticisms, if any, have been directed against the police in your country?

Example

The police in my country are generally viewed positively. People feel grateful to them because they catch dangerous criminals and put them in prison, making the rest of us safer. Moreover, they put themselves in danger while doing their jobs. Many criminals have guns, and the police are always in danger of getting seriously hurt or killed when confronting criminals. Citizens feel that the police deserve gratitude for this.

My Paragraph

Unit 11 · Health & Medicine

Reading 1 A Real Cure for Insomnia

BEFORE YOU READ

Talk about these questions with your classmates.

1 What do you think are the most serious effects of not getting enough sleep? Brainstorm three effects with your partner.
2 Sleeping pills can have good and bad effects. Brainstorm one possible benefit and one possible drawback of taking sleeping pills.

Think About It

What do you think are the main causes of sleep problems?

VOCABULARY PREVIEW

Fill in the blanks with the words in the box. Change the form of the word if necessary.

route	establish	alternative	method	involve

1 This is the best way out of the three ______________ plans.

2 He ______________ a running club in the city.

3 The course ______________ a lot of class time and hard work.

4 Many people think her teaching ______________ are great for students.

5 We took the wrong ______________ to the hotel so now we are lost.

A Real Cure for Insomnia 21

by Charles N. Reilly, M.D.

We all know what it feels like to get less sleep than we need. All-nighters of studying or partying can mess up our routines for sure. But it usually only takes another good night's sleep to get us back on track. Yet for some people, it isn't so easy.

A comfortable environment is an important part of getting a good night's sleep.

A colleague of mine during my residency work at New York Hospital Queens could never seem to get enough sleep. She often came in to work exhausted and would complain of having spent the night tossing and turning[1] in her bed. It affected not only her work, but her memory and relationships with others as well. On one frightening occasion, it almost caused her to make a fatal[2] mistake during a surgery. Despite my assertion[3] that sleeping medications did more harm than good, she decided to try drug therapy for her sleeplessness. But I can't blame her. She was at her wit's end[4].

C What claim about sleep medications did the author make to the woman? Underline it.

As a doctor, I understand the value of drugs. There are many health conditions for which drugs are the only answer. In this case, however, it isn't clear how beneficial sleeping aids really are, especially when compared to the **alternative**. Cognitive Behavioral Therapy, or CBT, is a more effective and less harmful **method** of treating sleeplessness.

Q What does the author think is a better treatment for sleeplessness? Circle it.

Once she started taking sleep medications, my colleague noticed an improvement in her ability to fall asleep and stay asleep. But no one should take sleeping aids for more than a few days, or a few weeks at the most. Sleeping pills can be highly addictive[5]. Once the meds are stopped, they can lead to an even worse case of insomnia than the patient had before. To make matters worse, the quality of sleep, as my colleague discovered, isn't as good as natural sleep, and leaves you feeling sleepy the next day.

C The author makes a recommendation. Underline it.

CBT, on the other hand, presents no such danger. The components of CBT **involve** forming healthy behaviors and environments, or "sleep hygiene," which are most helpful to habitual[6], natural sleep. Having a cool bedroom, avoiding caffeine and exercise at night, and developing relaxing habits before bed are all examples of good sleep hygiene. By practicing such behaviors, people **establish** sleeping habits that work indefinitely,[7] rather than for just a few weeks.

1 **toss and turn** *idiom* to not sleep well
2 **fatal** *adj.* causing death
3 **assertion** *n.* a claim or statement
4 **be at (one's) wit's end** *idiom* to be very upset and not know what to do
5 **addictive** *adj.* creating a strong and harmful need for something
6 **habitual** *adj.* occurring regularly
7 **indefinitely** *adv.* continuing with no fixed end

In addition to being addictive, sleeping pills also have a negative effect on overall health. Dr. Daniel Kripke, co-director of research at Scripps Clinic in San Diego, found in a study of 10,500 people taking sleeping pills that the prolonged[8] use of such meds led to a thirty-five percent higher risk of cancer. Dr. Kripke claimed that people taking sleeping pills regularly have an even greater risk of developing lymphoma, lung, and other cancers than do people who smoke. His study also found that patients taking sleep medications were more than four times as likely to have died during the 2.5-year follow-up study as those who did not take the drugs.

Q Circle two negative effects of sleeping pills found in the study.

While it's true that sleeping pills do provide relatively fast relief of the problem, the relief is short-lived and involves proven long-term risks. On the other hand, CBT requires time and effort to become effective but has no negative effects in the long run. Restriction therapy—a component of CBT which includes cutting out naps and putting off bedtime until late at night—may require up to six weeks to have a positive effect on the patient. The patient is also encouraged to identify habits that might have been preventing sleep. Dr. Donn Posner, director of Behavioral Sleep Medicine at Lifespan Hospitals in Rhode Island, recommends changing these habits. He instructs his patients not to spend time in the bedroom or on the bed unless it's time to go to sleep. He also recommends avoiding exercise or working before bed as it can excite the patient to the point where he or she cannot relax.

Q Circle a possible drawback of CBT.

Patients who undergo CBT are encouraged to keep sleep diaries.

Another clear advantage of CBT over drug therapy is a doctor's ability to individualize respective treatments. Whereas drug formulas cannot be personalized for each patient, CBT treatment can. My colleague's sleep diary—detailing all of her habits and quirks[9]—allowed her doctors to prescribe[10] treatments that were exclusive[11] to her condition.

Of course, creating new habits is time-consuming and difficult. But the upside[12] is that once the good habits are formed, they can be kept up indefinitely with no negative side effects. I'm happy to say that after my colleague tried (and failed) the drug therapy **route**, she went for the healthier CBT option. She is now on the road to permanent relief from her condition—something drug therapy was never able to offer her.

Q Underline at least three advantages of CBT over drug therapy.

8 **prolonged** *adj.* lengthy; continued
9 **quirk** *n.* a unique personal characteristic
10 **prescribe** *v.* (of a doctor) to tell somebody what medicine to take
11 **exclusive** *adj.* unique
12 **upside** *n.* a benefit

READING COMPREHENSION

A **Choose the best answer according to the reading.**

1 Based on paragraph 3, which statement would the author most likely agree with?

a. More research must be done on CBT to prove its effectiveness.
b. In general, doctors should not prescribe drugs for their patients.
c. Drugs should be avoided if an effective alternative treatment exists.
d. The best way to cure patients' sleeplessness is to prescribe medication.

2 Based on the passage, what is NOT a negative effect of taking sleeping pills?

a. They result in a low quality of sleep.
b. They increase people's consumption of caffeinated drinks.
c. People who take them for too long may require them in order to sleep.
d. They have been shown to increase the chances of getting diseases.

3 In what way are CBT patients involved in their own treatment routines?

a. They only take medications when they feel it is necessary.
b. They compare their sleep diaries to those of other patients.
c. They only drink caffeinated drinks in the morning.
d. They identify the things that might prevent them from sleeping.

B **Below is the beginning of a summary of the passage. Complete the passage summary by writing the correct sentences in the table. Two of the choices will not be used. They are either minor details or incorrect facts.**

Not all cures for insomnia are the same.	
CBT • •	Drug therapy • •

a. Doctors create sleep diaries to record the sleep habits of their patients.
b. Prolonged sleeping pill use has been shown to produce a thirty-five percent increase in cancer.
c. Improvements in sleep that result from CBT tend to be permanent.
d. Drug therapy has the advantage of providing a speedy short-term cure.
e. CBT, which requires behavioral changes, has no major negative effects.
f. Drug therapy can seriously damage a person's health in a number of ways.

SUMMARY

Fill in the blanks with the phrases in the box.

time and effort	highly addictive	"sleep hygiene"
lower-quality sleep	sleep diary	risk of addiction

Treatments for Insomnia: Comparison

Sleeping Pills	• Work quickly • Provide only short-term benefits and ❶ ________________ • Can be ❷ ________________ • Possible links to cancer and other diseases • Cannot be individualized for each patient
Cognitive Behavioral Therapy	• Requires ❸ ________________ to be effective • Provides a long-term solution by establishing healthy ❹ ________________ • No ❺ ________________ • No links to disease • Can be individualized with the help of a ❻ ________________

DISCUSSION

Discuss the following questions with your partner or classmates.

1 There are many sleeping medications available. Why do you suppose this is so?

2 If you had trouble sleeping, would you rather try drug therapy or CBT? Why?

WRITING

Write a short paragraph answering the following question.

Q: What are some of the main causes of sleeplessness, and how can people solve the problem?

☐ **[Opinion]** The leading causes of sleeplessness include too much work and __________. People can solve the problem by changing their behavior.

Example

The leading causes of sleeplessness include too much work and too much caffeine. People can solve the problem by changing their behavior. The most common cause of sleeplessness is the fact that people are just too busy. As a student, I seldom get to bed before midnight. Sadly, my parents suffer from the same problem because of the demands of their jobs. This in turn causes another problem. To help them stay awake for long hours, many people drink a lot of coffee. This only makes the problem of sleeplessness worse. The caffeine keeps people awake when they go to bed, which means they are more tired the next day. Some people think that sleeping pills provide a quick fix for the problem. But the harmful effects of taking these pills over the long run have been documented in a number of clinical studies. So pills are not the answer. Changing behavior just might work. To start with, people need to cut back on caffeine consumption. But the real cure will only come after people evaluate their work schedules. We must evaluate our schedules and our priorities in general so that we can change our behavior. By doing this, we can finally solve the serious problem of sleeplessness.

My Paragraph

Unit 11 • Health & Medicine

Reading 2 The Uncommon Cold

BEFORE YOU READ

Talk about these questions with your classmates.

1 What causes a cold?
2 What can you do to protect yourself from colds?

VOCABULARY PREVIEW

Fill in the blanks with the words in the box. Change the form of the word if necessary.

accelerate	antibodies	spray	molecular	nasty

1 One challenge in organ transplantation is that a patient's ________________ may attack the organ as if it were an infection.

2 Anyone who has ever experienced a(n) ________________ paper cut knows how painful they can be.

3 You can buy this perfume either as a lotion or as a(n) ________________.

4 ________________ biology is the study of physiological processes at the most fundamental level of elements and compounds.

5 Microwave ovens are convenient because they ________________ the cooking process.

The Uncommon Cold 22

Why can't we just make a common cold vaccine?

Catching colds is a common complaint for people all over the world. While even a **nasty** cold won't kill you, no one enjoys the accompanying symptoms[1]: a sore scratchy throat, runny nose, constant sneezing, and headaches. Colds are uncomfortable and often inconvenient, usually lasting about seven days but often lingering for up to fourteen days. On average, human adults contract between two and five colds annually, while children catch as many as six to ten.

It's no surprise that developing and selling cold medication has become big business for pharmaceutical[2] companies. Each year, consumers spend billions of dollars on medicines to alleviate this recurring problem. From over-the-counter[3] remedies to expensive prescription[4] products, they are more than happy to hand over money for something that could help **accelerate** a recovery. The irony is that most available medicines are only palliatives, meaning they may help relieve cold symptoms but do not cure the illness itself.

The fact is that currently there is no cure available for the common cold. Not even a suitable vaccine has been developed. In the case of influenza, commonly known as the flu, vaccines[5] do exist, and getting one yearly is recommended. By contrast, the reason that a cold is so hard to vaccinate against or cure is because it isn't caused by any single disease. There are actually about 200 viruses responsible for our cold symptoms. In other words, a cold may not necessarily be as "common" as you imagine.

Each cold virus carries specific antigens, substances that trigger immune responses. Immune responses cause our bodies to create protective proteins called **antibodies** to fight off harmful diseases. So far it has proved impossible to create one vaccine that can produce the disparate[6] antibodies required to fight so many different antigens. Another problem is that cold viruses have the ability to change their **molecular** structure—in other words, to undergo mutations. That means that even if a suitable vaccine were developed, cold viruses could alter in a relatively short space of time, making the vaccine obsolete[7]. Even flu vaccines, which target a specific, known virus, must be updated frequently for this reason.

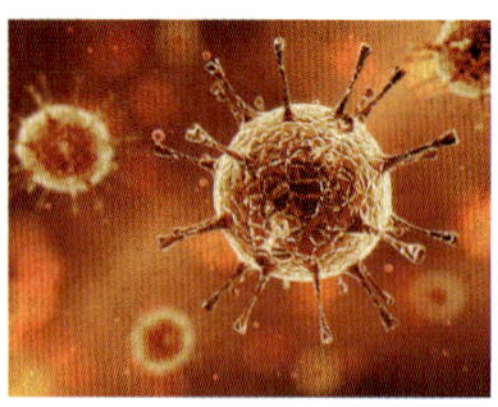

Colds are caused by viruses.

1	**symptom**	*n.* a characteristic sign of illness
2	**pharmaceutical**	*adj.* related to the preparation of chemicals for medical use
3	**over-the-counter**	*adj.* sold legally without a doctor's permission
4	**prescription**	*n.* a note from a doctor stating what medicine you need
5	**vaccine**	*n.* a medicine that helps build resistance to disease
6	**disparate**	*adj.* not alike; cannot be compared
7	**obsolete**	*adj.* no longer produced or used; out of date

Pharmaceutical companies often invest millions of dollars in clinical trials.

In the last two decades, medical research has concentrated on developing medicines to fight a family of viruses called the rhinoviruses, which are responsible for causing about thirty-five percent of all colds. In the late 1990s, researchers seemed to have some initial success with an anti-viral molecule called BIRR4. This substance appeared to prevent rhinoviruses from binding with cells in our noses, thus blocking an infection—if taken just before getting sick. Unfortunately, people don't know when they are about to catch a cold, so they wouldn't have known when to take the BIRR4. As a result, research into the product was dropped in 2000.

Between 1997 and 2001, a company called ViroPharma tried to get approval to market an antiviral drug called pleconaril which worked in a similar way to BIRR4. Studies indicated that pleconaril prevented rhinoviruses from attaching themselves to human cells by binding with the outer shell of the viral molecules. An application to commercialize an oral form of pleconaril was turned down by the Federal Drug Administration in the USA. The reason given was that the safety and efficacy[8] of the drug had not been proven in a convincing manner.

Q Underline the reason the FDA rejected pleconaril in 2002.

ViroPharma decided to carry on with research and developed a pleconaril nasal spray. They believed this to be an improved version, which could be used to combat colds and asthma. In 2003, the pharmaceutical giant Schering Plough entered into an agreement with ViroPharma giving Schering Plough an option to license and market the spray to prevent cold viruses from exacerbating asthma. By 2007, pleconaril spray had undergone its second phase of clinical trials[9]. As of 2015, the results of these trials have not been released, but according to Schering Plough, pleconaril is still under development.

For now, perhaps the safest way to fight a cold is simply to follow conventional wisdom: get plenty of bed rest, take over-the-counter remedies to combat symptoms, and drink plenty of fluids. If you do these things, your cold should be gone in seven days. Or do absolutely nothing, and it should be gone within a couple of weeks.

Q What are two measures you can take at home without using any medicine?

8	**efficacy**	*n.* effectiveness; how well something works
9	**clinical trial**	*n.* a test that checks the safety and effectiveness of a treatment

READING COMPREHENSION

A **Mark each statement as true (*T*) or false (*F*) according to the reading.**

1 ______ One of the usual symptoms of a cold is a fever.

2 ______ Children contract two to five colds each year on average.

3 ______ Many colds are caused by rhinoviruses.

4 ______ Pleconaril spray cold medicine is now available in pharmacies.

5 ______ Getting plenty of rest and drinking liquids are really the only things that alleviate cold symptoms.

B **Choose the best answer according to the reading.**

1 What is the main idea of the reading?

a. In spite of extensive research, there is still no cure for the common cold.
b. Soon the drug pleconaril will cure all types of colds.
c. BIRR4 was a poorly designed medication.
d. Children are more affected by colds than adults.

2 The word they in paragraph 2 refers to ______.

a. products
b. consumers
c. remedies
d. companies

3 What was the problem with BIRR4?

a. It was an effective anti-viral medication.
b. It prevented rhinoviruses from binding to cells in our noses.
c. It only worked if people took it before getting sick.
d. All of the above.

4 Which is a reason why it is difficult to create a cold vaccine?

a. Researchers are unsure how colds are spread.
b. Vaccines are only effective if taken before getting a cold.
c. The cold viruses are able to undergo mutations.
d. Previous vaccines were shown to be unsafe.

SUMMARY

An introductory sentence for a brief summary of the passage is provided below. Select THREE more sentences to complete the summary.

First Sentence: While the common cold won't kill you, the symptoms can make everyday life very difficult.

1. Pleconaril, a nasal spray developed by ViroPharm and Schering Plough, could become a preventative medication for colds and asthma.
2. Commercialization of BIRR4 dropped in 2000 because it was obsolete.
3. Colds can linger anywhere from one to two weeks, and the symptoms accompanying them can include fevers and sneezing.
4. The cold medicine industry is big business; however, these medications only address symptoms and don't prevent the virus.
5. It is nearly impossible to create a cold vaccine due to the number of viruses that can cause colds and their ability to undergo mutations.
6. Vaccines exist for the flu, and getting one every year is recommended.

DISCUSSION

Discuss the following questions with your partner or classmates.

1 Do you think there will ever be a cure for the cold?

2 Besides medication, what ways of fighting cold symptoms have you heard about? Do they work?

WRITING

Write a short paragraph answering the following questions.

1 What do you usually do when you're feeling sick? Do you do anything other than take medicine?
2 Have you heard of any other alternative remedies for colds? Do you think they work?

Example

I think alternative cold remedies are not as good as medicines. Any alternative remedies, such as tea with honey, never worked for me. While I have tried some different types of alternative remedies, regular medicine always helps me when I am sick. Also, cold medicines have been thoroughly scientifically tested and have been proven effective. The same cannot be said of alternative remedies.

My Paragraph

Unit 12 • Urban Life & Environment

Reading 1 Buy Locally? Not If You Care about the Environment

BEFORE YOU READ

Talk about these questions with your classmates.

This blog post is about buying food only from local sources. The author gives her opinion about this practice, which is becoming popular in some countries. What are some possible disadvantages of buying only food that is produced locally?

VOCABULARY PREVIEW

Choose the one that is closest to the meaning of the word in bold.

1 Another shopper **assured** me that the tomato that I was holding was excellent.
a. denied b. assumed c. promised

2 The economist Steve Sexton created a **theoretical** world in which all food was locally produced.
a. perfect b. imaginary c. confusing

3 When the crops are ready, they must be harvested and sent to a **distributor**.
a. supplier b. farmer c. customer

4 Locally-grown vegetables are a better **purchase** than those that are shipped from far away.
a. bought goods b. food c. technology

5 The **transit** of produce from Africa to England does not create huge carbon emissions.
a. movement b. elimination c. consumption

Buy Locally? Not If You Care about the Environment

by Nancy Sullivan

Just yesterday, I came across a local farmers' market as I took a new route home from the office. I'd forgotten that this market takes place every week, and consequently spent a bit of time wandering[1] from stall[2] to stall, taking in the sights and smells of the fresh produce[3].

Farmers' markets are popular in large cities.

While there, I started talking with another shopper and suggested that I could buy produce of similar quality at a supermarket for much less money. She **assured** me that the tomato I was squeezing was the best **purchase** I could ever make. I'd be supporting local farmers, and I'd be helping the environment, too. And, with a flash of anger in her eyes, she said that I wouldn't be "enriching the evil corporate agricultural machine." Seriously–she actually said that.

I set the tomato down and backed away slowly.

It's easy to believe that buying locally-produced food is better than buying food at a grocery store. After all, you get to meet the people who (supposedly) grew the food you're buying. You know exactly where your food is coming from. But I left the market that day feeling that a little research was needed.

A number of problems became clear immediately. First, there's no real definition of "local" when it comes to talking about a food's origin. The idea of eating local is so appealing to some people that one enthusiastic eater even coined[4] the term "locavore" to describe someone who only eats food grown within a certain radius[5]. But what distance are we talking about here? It could mean a 250-mile or even 500-mile radius, with no real way to determine when it stops being "local" and starts being "imported."

Another problem—different seasons and locations yield different crops. California has a better climate for growing strawberries and grapes, while Idaho has better conditions for growing potatoes. Does that mean only Californians should have the benefit of eating farm-fresh strawberries? Of course not. Why would a farmer in California try to compete with one in Idaho by growing potatoes if his or her land and climate are better suited for growing something else?

Q What is the second drawback of buying only locally-produced food that the author mentions?

C What is the source of the author's information? Do you think that this source is reliable?

In his *Freakonomics* article entitled "The Inefficiency of Local Food," Steve Sexton invents a **theoretical** world in which all food production is localized. In this system, food producers in each state would have to grow a share of produce proportional to that

1 **wander** *v.* to walk around with no fixed destination
2 **stall** *n.* a table at which items are sold, often in a market
3 **produce** *n.* fresh fruit and vegetables
4 **coin** *v.* to create a new word or phrase
5 **radius** *n.* a round area that covers a particular distance from a central point

state's population, rather than mass-producing a crop to export elsewhere.

Sexton followed the steps involved in farming and estimated the costs of a locavore system. To start, you'd have to get your hands on more farmland. Farming requires vast amounts of space, which has to come from somewhere. In this case, it would come from the existing habitats of wild plants and animals. After the land has been cleared, the crops need fertilizer and chemicals to ensure that the plants remain healthy and undamaged. Next, the crops have to be harvested and moved to a **distributor**. Finally, the food would have to be moved to a store.

Q Why could a locavore system disrupt plant and animal habitats? Underline the information.

According to Sexton's estimates, this local system would require 60 million additional acres of farmland, 2.7 million tons more fertilizer, and 50 million pounds more chemicals when compared to our current production and distribution systems. The environmental impact would be utterly[6] devastating, destroying habitats and increasing pollution.

Container ships can carry large amounts of produce across the seas.

While supporters of locally grown food will argue that transporting food for long distances increases carbon emissions, Dr. Alexander Kasterine of the International Trade Centre suggests the opposite. Let's look at pineapples and mangoes, for example. Of course, you could grow them in hothouses in the UK. But farms in England, as it turns out, use more energy in their food production than do farmers in Africa, who rely less on tractors and machinery and more on manual labor. **Transit** from Africa actually results in lower carbon emissions than would growing the food at home and transporting it a shorter distance. On top of that, purposefully avoiding buying the agricultural output of developing nations would be unfair to the farmers in those countries. The solution, Dr. Kasterine says, is not to grow locally and cut off the food supply from overseas, but to focus on reducing carbon emissions at home.

C What is the author's purpose for writing this paragraph?
(1) To refute a popular belief
(2) To support the locavore's stance
(3) To compare various farming techniques

OK, you ask, what about growing your own food? Community gardens are popping up like weeds in urban areas thanks to initiatives from politicians, but I was surprised to find out that even growing your own vegetables doesn't have as positive an impact as you'd think. In places like New York City, where space is already scarce[7] and expensive, putting aside acres of land for planting a few vegetables instead of developing housing forces more people outside city limits to where they're no longer in walking distance to work. Sustaining a dense population within a small area, where people can walk and take public transportation, does more good for the environment than planting a few rows of squash does.

Q What does the author say is environmentally better than growing your own food in urban areas?

We are thus faced with a dilemma[8]. Vast quantities of fossil fuels are consumed whether we ship our produce in from half a world away or grow it in empty city lots or small farms just outside of town. But if you crunch the numbers[9], the lesser of these two evils becomes apparent—at the end of the day, shipping in food is our best, if imperfect, choice over the long haul[10].

---

6 **utterly** *adv.* completely; totally
7 **scarce** *adj.* very limited in number or amount; rare
8 **dilemma** *n.* a problem without a good solution
9 **crunch numbers** *idiom* to perform a mathematical computation
10 **over the long haul** *idiom* over a long period of time; in the long run

READING COMPREHENSION

A **Organize the ideas from the reading. Review the passage and fill in the graphic organizer below.**

Should we only buy locally-produced food?

Locavore system seems like a good idea:
- Supports local [1] ________________
- Helps the environment

Problems with locavore system:
- No clear definition of "[2] ________________"
- Different seasons and locations yield different crops
- Needs more [3] ________________ (60 million acres)
- Requires more [4] ________________ (2.7 million tons) and more chemicals (50 million pounds)

Problems with community gardens:
- Scarcity of urban land
- Land better used for [5] ________________

Conclusion:
- Better to [6] ________________ than to grow locally

B **Choose the best answer according to the reading.**

1 What can be inferred from paragraph 5 about some of the produce that is advertised as "local"?

a. It could have been grown on a farm in a foreign country.
b. It might not be as healthful as food that is imported from far away.
c. It does not fit the accepted definition of the word "locavore."
d. It required a significant amount of fuel to reach the consumer.

2 Which of the following is NOT mentioned in paragraph 9 as a result of the theorized locavore system?

a. Increased acreage needs
b. Negative impact on wildlife
c. Use of organic fertilizers
d. Greater chemical requirements

SUMMARY

Fill in the blanks with the phrases in the box.

meet the people	chemicals and fertilizers	public transportation
existing habitats	for corporations	uses less energy

Pros

- Provides support for local farmers rather than ❶ ______________
- Allows you to ❷ ______________ who grow your food
- Transporting food long distance takes fuel, causes emissions

Cons

- Certain crops are limited to certain areas and seasons
- Requires the clearing of ❸ ______________ for more farmland
- Involves use of more ❹ ______________
- Shipping food from some regions (e.g. Africa) ❺ ______________
- Community gardens reduce space for housing → less use of ❻ ______________

DISCUSSION

A Read the excerpt from the reading passage.

Buy Locally? Not If You Care about the Environment

In his *Freakonomics* article entitled "The Inefficiency of Local Food," Steve Sexton invents a theoretical world in which all food production is localized. In this system, food producers in each state would have to grow a share of produce proportional to that state's population, rather than mass-producing a crop to export elsewhere.

B Discuss the following questions with your partner or classmates.

1. What would happen if your country could not import any food?
2. How might it affect the population?
3. Would more farmland be needed? What might happen to the land?
4. Can you think of any other ways that your country might be affected?

WRITING

Write a short paragraph answering the following question.

Q: Is it better to buy locally-produced food or food that is imported from far away?

☐ **[Opinion 1]** For a number of reasons, it is better to buy locally-produced food than imported food.

☐ **[Opinion 2]** Without a doubt, it makes more sense to buy imported food than locally grown food.

Example

For a number of reasons, it's better to buy locally-produced food than imported food. Of course, food that comes from nearby small farms is often quite expensive compared to imported food. But the benefits outweigh this minor drawback. The first benefit is taste. Few people could argue that imported food tastes as good as locally-produced food. For example, you can buy strawberries year-round at the supermarket. These berries lack taste and are often not even red! But the strawberries sold at local farmers' markets in the summer are bright red, juicy, and delicious! The environmental benefits are even more important than the taste. In their article "Living on the 100-Mile Diet," the authors reveal that the average American meal uses up to seventeen times more petroleum in transit than a locally-produced meal does. In the end, it's worth the extra cost to eat locally-produced food. It's both tastier and less damaging to the environment than imported food.

My Paragraph

Reading 2 Urban Design: The Need for Green Spaces

BEFORE YOU READ

Talk about these questions with your classmates.

What are some of the benefits of having green spaces in cities? Make a list of them and share it with a partner.

VOCABULARY PREVIEW

Choose the one that is closest to the meaning of the word in bold.

1 The city's **infrastructure** is a mix of concrete structures and green spaces.
a. road system b. basic structures c. underground pipes

2 The study looked at various forms of **misconduct** that residents committed.
a. offense b. behavior c. investigation

3 Residents have a greater **appreciation** for the area they live in if it has green spaces.
a. gratitude b. neglect c. awareness

4 The **revolution** of ideas for new types of green spaces is spreading across the country.
a. rotation b. major remodeling c. major change

5 People need a way to **offset** the hard urban landscape with greenery.
a. approve b. balance c. redirect

Urban Design: The Need for Green Spaces

24

by Jon Maes / Language Cradle Consulting

Q What are some effects of green spaces on learning and working environments? Underline them.

The University of Guelph-Humber in Toronto, Canada, is gaining recognition in the world of academia[1] because of its indoor "living wall." Students, employees, and visitors to the campus praise the four-story plant construction for its visual appeal and ingenuity[2]. In fact, the university's decision to build the living wall coincides with studies that show the positive impacts green spaces have on learning and working environments. For example, scientific data indicates that plants enhance student and employee satisfaction, which results in decreased absenteeism[3] and increased productivity.

Q What does the author say city planners need to do?

Greenery has positive effects on learning and working environments.

The positive impact of greenery on school environments is only one aspect of the green **revolution** that has been taking place over the past few decades. Increasingly, green spaces are changing the character of cities and enriching[4] people's lives in various ways. However, not everyone agrees. The challenge now is to persuade all city planners to **offset** the concrete coldness of many downtown neighborhoods with areas of greenery, such as parks, gardens, and arboretums[5].

Unfortunately, the sections of cities that have the greatest need for greenery are also the places where it is most difficult to find room for it. City planners then must be creative and inventive when incorporating greenery into existing **infrastructures**.

Green roofs are an innovation that is becoming more commonplace in major cities. A famous green roof in the US is found on top of the Chicago City Hall. It covers an area of 20,300 square feet with native plants from the Midwest region. There is also the International Hall in Fukuoka, Japan. This government building is made up of fifteen terraces[6] with 35,000 plants representing seventy-six different species.

Q What innovation does Parkhill in Bratislava share with Chicago and Fukuoka?

Another example is an award-winning design in Bratislava, Slovakia, called the Parkhill. Architects were given the task of meeting the city's need for more housing and public spaces without taking away the urban forest surrounding the city center. Their solution made use of green roofs similar to those in Chicago and Fukuoka and included courtyards and vertical gardens along with 350 apartments, dozens of offices, and a hotel—all built on the hillside.

Green spaces do more than just create better learning and working environments.

1 **academia** *n.* the community concerned with the pursuit of knowledge and study

2 **ingenuity** *n.* the quality or instance of being very smart; cleverness

3 **absenteeism** *n.* repeated absence from a place where regular attendance is required, such as work or school

4 **enrich** *v.* to make more interesting, important, or rewarding

5 **arboretum** *n.* a place where trees are grown for study or display

6 **terrace** *n.* a flat, raised section of ground

They offer many other advantages for cities and the environment. Certain plants act as natural filters by removing chemicals and toxins from the air. Plants also help decrease indoor temperatures by blocking out the sun. They can even protect external walls from weather damage. Building owners should be happy to hear this. Think of the savings they can make. Moreover, plants provide a habitat for birds, squirrels, and other urban wildlife.

C What does the author infer about building owners with regard to green spaces?

Additionally, in cities that receive heavy rainfall, vegetation absorbs some of the water and prevents sewer systems from becoming overloaded. And because leaves have the ability to trap sound, plants can act as a noise reducer, so having green spaces in densely-populated areas helps muffle[7] street noise.

Experts have also found a connection between the amount of greenery in the environment and crime rates. Green spaces, it seems, decrease stress, anxiety, and aggression in people, which in turn leads to a reduction in the occurrence of violence. Indeed, a study of apartments by the city of Chicago found that greenery can lessen crime by as much as fifty percent, including littering[8], vandalism[9], and other acts of criminal **misconduct**. Part of the reason for this reduction is that residents have more **appreciation** for the area they live in. Green areas also attract people to go there, and the large number of potential eyewitnesses can be a deterrent to criminals.

In addition to reducing crime, green spaces can actually support the local economy. Research from the University of Washington indicates that shopping districts with trees and gardens are more appealing to customers. In particular, surveys determined that customers spent 9 to 12 percent more time in shopping districts with greenery than in those without. Psychologically, landscaping[10] also has the effect of making people think that the quality of goods and services is higher because of the impression that extra attention is being given to the shopping environment. This results in more shopping and more buying, which is sure to make any store owner happy.

Q How can green spaces help the local economy?

All in all, the importance of having green spaces in public areas is becoming increasingly clear. As human populations grow, cities expand, which exerts pressure on the natural surroundings. City planners should find innovative ways of building green spaces into urban designs because the benefits to our society and the environment are too great to ignore. With such impressive green spaces serving as models, it will be interesting to see how people will use nature to transform cities in the future.

7 **muffle** *v.* to make quieter by using a covering of some sort

8 **littering** *n.* a type of crime involving trash being scattered in public places instead of being properly disposed of

9 **vandalism** *n.* a type of crime involving purposeful damage to property

10 **landscape** *v.* to change a piece of land by adding plants and other features to make it more attractive

READING COMPREHENSION

Choose the best answer according to the reading.

1 What is the passage mainly about?

a. City planning as it relates to environmental protection
b. The reasons that modern cities must have green spaces
c. Considerations for planting vegetation indoors and outdoors
d. The use of natural environments in award-winning urban designs

2 All of the following are advantages of green spaces mentioned in the passage EXCEPT:

a. helping the local economy by creating jobs
b. providing homes for native animals
c. reducing flooding in places with heavy rainfall
d. deterring residents from committing crimes

3 According to the passage, what is one way that having green spaces can reduce crime?

a. It gives people more places to hide from violent criminals in their neighborhood.
b. It helps the local economy, so people have more money.
c. It attracts more people to the area, so criminals are more worried about getting caught.
d. It creates more activities for people to participate in so they do not cause trouble.

4 Which of the following statements about shoppers would the author most likely agree with?

a. They are more concerned about prices than the landscaping.
b. They notice when store owners decorate their stores with greenery.
c. They are more likely to visit shopping areas that have green spaces.
d. They tend to shop near their homes regardless of the urban design.

5 How can plants help protect buildings?

a. By absorbing the water that does not soak into the ground
b. By protecting the walls from overexposure to sunlight
c. By decreasing the amount of litter in the area
d. By keeping animals away

SUMMARY

Fill in the blanks with the phrases in the box.

natural filters	increase satisfaction	protects walls
chemicals and toxins	green roofs	stress and anxiety

Green Spaces in Urban Areas

Problem

- Cold appearance of many urban areas
- Need for more housing and public spaces (e.g. Bratislava)
  ❶ ________________ in the air
- Heavy rainfall and other severe weather
- ❷ ________________ lead to crime
- Slow economy

↓

Solution

- Plants ❸ ________________ and productivity
- Use of ❹ ________________ and vertical gardens
- Plants act as ❺ ________________
- Vegetation absorbs water, keeps temperatures down, and
  ❻ ________________
- Green spaces help people relax
- Green spaces lead to more shopping and spending

DISCUSSION

Discuss the following questions with your partner or classmates.

1 Do you agree with the author's argument that green spaces can help reduce crime? Why or why not?

2 What are some possible disadvantages of building green spaces in cities? Explain.

WRITING

Write a short paragraph answering the following question.

Q: You are a mayor and must decide how to use some empty space near City Hall. In your opinion, which of the following would be the best use of the space?

Example

In my town, we already have plenty of parks and houses. So I would create an urban garden and ask the citizens to help plant it and maintain it. This would be a great way to bring people in the area together. We could use the food for a good cause. For example, we could feed the homeless or the poor with the vegetables that we grow.

My Paragraph

MEMO

Memo

Memo

MEMO